IN SPITE *of* ME

In Spite of Me
A Memoir

Copyright © 2025 Eldred Sawyer

This book is set in the typeface *Athelas* designed by Veronika Burian and Jose Scaglione.

Paperback ISBN: 978-1-967262-30-4
Hardcover ISBN: 979-8-3496-7868-4

A Publication of *Tall Pine Books*
PO Box 42 Warsaw | Indiana 46581
www.tallpinebooks.com

| 1 25 25 20 16 02 |

Published in the United States of America

IN SPITE of ME

ELDRED SAWYER

I'd like to dedicate *In Spite of Me* first to my precious wife, Jeanmarie. I know I couldn't have done this without her by my side—her steadfast encouragement, her ability to abound and abase, always keeping the bigger picture in mind. Her fierce maternal love for our children. Her ongoing willingness to sacrifice without complaining. She always rejected the "what about me" question, almost to a fault. I know that because she played mostly a behind-the-scenes role, many will be surprised when eternity reveals her true significance in this story.

And to our children—Merideth, Jeri Quinn, Lonnie, Rebekah, Caleb, Naomi, and Dannah—who paid a price they never volunteered to pay. Beyond the physical sacrifices of the early years, there was the sacrifice of privacy: little things like having a phone at the table on the rare occasions we had dinner together. Sharing your parents with so many who never had their own. Loving me through my learning curve of being a dad and husband—an ongoing process to this day. One of the most fascinating things to me is the uniqueness of each of you. Like a fingerprint or DNA, you are all so beautifully different, and because of that, you each hold a unique place in my heart and have earned a deep appreciation and respect from me simply for being you.

I love you all.

But yeah—Naomi is my favorite. Bahaha! (Family joke.)

Contents

Endorsements

When we were first introduced to Eldred Sawyer, he looked unhealthy and undernourished. He was described by those who knew him from the streets as *just plain mean!* One man told my wife, Sharon, "If Eldred Sawyer was walking down the street, I would cross to the other side!"

People who knew the *"mean"* Eldred were amazed by the radical change in his life. Hiding under his tough exterior was a man with a very tender heart. From a world of violence, crime, and people who are resistant to authority, Eldred was in search of a father. He was looking for direction for his life and eager to be under authority. Thankfully, Leonard Brannon devoted himself to helping Eldred, in part by bringing him to church and Overcomers meetings.

We had learned to be skeptical of the motives of recovering addicts because so many asked for money. Some needs were legitimate, for food and shelter, but most just wanted money for drugs or alcohol.

Sharon and I, along with church leaders, recognized Eldred's sincerity. His leadership skills were obvious, and several Overcomers group members eagerly followed him.

I gave Eldred the keys to a church van and my personal

credit card for gas to deliver an expensive TV camera to a drug-infested area where we were shooting a video. It never entered my mind that I could not trust Eldred. He later told me he was surprised and encouraged—surprised that I trusted him with such expensive equipment that could be hocked and a credit card with a large limit that he could exploit.

There came a time when Eldred and Leonard Brannon came to my office to ask the church for financial support, informing me they were going to start a food ministry for the poor. I wondered who had the greatest need, Eldred or those they wanted to help. Eldred's passion to help others was greater than his own personal needs. He did not seek a position of authority but sought to serve others. His heart was rooted in giving, just as it continues today.

–CHARLES AND SHARON BURTON
Founding Leaders, *Overcomers ministry*

I remember the day I got a call from a pastor in Kaufman, TX, concerning a young man and his two children needing a place to live. He told me the young man had a long time addiction to heroin and meth, was living in a drug house apartment strung out and needed help. I found out later that he had no intention of giving his life to the Lord but only wanted a safe place for his two children. But God had another plan.

From the moment Eldred Sawyer and his children showed up at our home, I knew that God had His hand on his life. I have worked with hundreds of men and women over the years, and only Eldred had the same heart, commitment, and passion for the poor and needy as myself.

The Apostle Paul said the same thing about Timothy: "He is the only one who shares my feelings and who really cares about you" (see Philippians 2:20).

From day one, Eldred stood by my side as we worked together to build CareCenter Ministries over the first seven years of the ministry. He had the same commitment, the same love, and the same passion for the forgotten ones of society.

I picked him up out of the pit of brokenness and bondage when no one would give him the "time of day." Then, several years later, he returned the "favor" and picked me up out of my pit of brokenness and despair. For that, I will be eternally grateful.

–LEONARD BRANNON

Co-Founder, *CareCenter Ministries*

What a joy it is for me to honor the life and continuing ministry of my dear friend and co-laborer Eldred Sawyer. As his pastor I gladly and thankfully watched the mighty hand of

God raise Eldred up and transform his life from faith to faith and glory to glory.

Now four decades later, the abundant fruit that abounds in and through Eldred's life and ministry will exceed beyond time into eternity!

Birthing multiple congregations, feeding and lifting the broken, while establishing Truth Academy, only begins to express the glorious blessing Eldred Sawyer is to so many. His reward before the Lord will be massive!

–Dr. Larry Lea
Pastor and Evangelist

Eldred Sawyer's story of redemption is a riveting miracle of grace. Not only was his rapid downward spiral stopped, his life was dramatically reversed. Since his encounter with Jesus Christ, Pastor Sawyer has lifted countless other lives through the power of the gospel. This message of hope will thrill your heart. Also, you will be challenged to offer your life to be used by God to lift others.

–David Shibley
Founder, *Global Advance*

Everyone has a vital story, but some stories are written in real time to encourage the hope of those who hear. Such is

Eldred's story. You can't hear it or read it without being challenged to believe God is both bigger and better than you thought. You will identify with the pain and the glory, and you will be better for it.

I am honored to be included in the elite list of Eldred Sawyer's friends. I am thrilled that his story is being told to a larger audience.

–DUDLEY HALL

Kerygma Ventures

When I first got to know Eldred Sawyer, he was assisting in CareCenter Ministries. He had just graduated from the Overcomer program himself and was eager to help others. After some time, I and three other senior pastors were asked to guide CareCenter Ministries through a leadership transition. We served as surrogate fathers to Eldred, helping prepare him for pastoral leadership.

I remember the day I left my own church to ordain Eldred Sawyer as the pastor of CareCenter Ministries. The Holy Spirit moved powerfully, and the mantle of leadership fell on him.

One story stands out. Pastor Gary Turner once encouraged Eldred in a time of deep financial despair and left his own Seiko watch on the table to remind Eldred not to give up ministry over something so small. Later, Eldred gave that same watch in a missions offering, and it eventually made its way back to me. I later gave it to Pastor Gary's son, Jerimy Turner, when I ordained him. The story of that watch is just one example of how Eldred's life and obedience have had generational impact.

–PASTOR C. GENE LEWIS
Senior Leader and Mentor

It's about time this story was told! The Eldred Sawyer story is a miracle narrative. His life could certainly make a fascinating stage play filled with both drama and humor. The truth here is often stranger than fiction.

Eldred grew up in the hard, fatherless world of Dallas's inner city. Yet by God's amazing grace, he has become a father to many. His ministry brings hope and promise to those whose lives were filled with dejection and addiction.

God must have a great sense of humor. He can take a street-savvy delinquent and turn him into a beloved leader of a well-known Christian ministry. Eldred's ministry has borne great fruit, rescuing the broken and messed up.

The secret? Eldred steadfastly depended on the Lord and the power of His Spirit.

–ROBERT SUMMERS
Pastor of *Prayer Mountain, Dallas*

In Spite of Me is the captivating life story of my dear friend, Eldred Sawyer. I wept, laughed and worshipped as I quickly turned the pages, riveted to the ancient and yet ever new testimony of the power of God's amazing grace. I encourage you to read this book and pass it on to others.

–SCOTT CAMP

President, *Valor Christian College (Columbus, OH)*

I have had the privilege of knowing Eldred Sawyer for over 30 years not only as a friend but as a co-laborer in the gospel.

His story is one of continual miracles.

From the miraculous salvaging by Christ of his broken life to becoming a vessel in the hands of God launching a multi-faceted ministry bringing help and hope to many.

This story will encourage you and underscore the truth that Jesus Christ changes lives today.

–SCOTT HINKLE

Evangelist, Author Dallas, TX

Wow! What a story, I was sent an advanced copy of Eldred's memoir and I picked it up and couldn't put it down. Read it all in one day. I love stories of redemption, grace and where the Lord gets all the glory. A prodigal son came home after years in the wilderness. Thank you to all the fathers in the faith who lead Eldred on his way to build a ministry to help the poor and destitute to find their way to Jesus. Thank you Jean Marie for standing by his side.

–SONNY CONATSER

President *Church on the Rock Network of Ministers*

This book chronicles the CareCenter Miracle! I've had the honor of walking with Eldred and Jeanmarie Sawyer alongside my wife, Nancy, for nearly four decades, and I've had a front-row seat to many of the life-changing stories you'll read here. They have never wavered in their faith, their love for God and people, or their commitment to the poor. Thousands upon thousands of lives have been shaped and transformed because of their courageous obedience to God.

William Booth of the Salvation Army once said, *"The greatness of a man's power is the measure of his surrender."* Eldred Sawyer is a great man by that measure. I have personally witnessed his journey—from a recovering heroin addict to a mighty modern-day apostle—living proof of what God can do with a fully surrendered life. His greatest strength has always been his unrelenting surrender to the call of God, and Jeanmarie has faithfully walked beside him every step of the way.

This book will inspire and motivate you to step beyond

a status quo life and into a life full of adventure and meaning. It will boost your faith, stir your heart, and challenge you to obey God courageously. If God could do it for Eldred and Jeanmarie, He can do it for you too. Get it. Read it. Do it.

–JOE MARTIN, JR.

Trinity Church Dallas

Foreword
by Pastor Terry Moore

I t is my honor to write the foreword for Eldred's story—a story I have walked beside since 1988. From the moment he stepped off the streets, a rough character with no pedigree or polished résumé, it was pretty clear that something rare was stirring in him. We began humbly, gathering at Browne's Café for Bible study, which marked the beginnings of what would become a movement.

Eldred started from the ground up . . . in fact, it's difficult to convey how truly "ground up" this was. Eldred had no fancy degree or institutional backing—just an unwavering faith in God and a heart for people. Yet from those raw beginnings grew outreach initiatives, men's and women's homes, and a church with multiple campuses. If I had to sum it all up in one word, it would be *miracle*.

I still remember the Thanksgiving outreach under the big tent. There were tents scattered around with volunteers who all sought to tackle different things—words of encouragement, physical healing, marriage issues, and so forth. The centerpiece was the *deliverance* tent. We figured that the volunteers in that particular tent might see a person or two over the course of the evening. The truth is, more souls pressed into that space than any other, because they came knowing they needed real, spiritual intervention. It wasn't just about food or shelter—it was about being set free.

And this perfectly illustrates the level of need that Eldred and Jean Marie have continually thrown themselves at for decades now.

The transformation of neighborhoods like lower East Dallas and Pleasant Grove stands as living proof: change begins in the spirit realm, then flows naturally into the streets. I remember when downtown investors first noticed the shift— they saw opportunity because the atmosphere had changed. I believe that Eldred and his team so shifted the atmosphere of the region that the prosperity these places now experience wouldn't have been feasible without their presence pioneering the way.

When that area became too cleaned up, Eldred simply moved deeper into a neighborhood with great need, planting again and watching the same spiritual watershed follow.

What makes the CareCenter unique isn't its buildings or programs—it's Christ. Discipleship is frontline. This is not an entry into a program; this is an invitation into a relationship with Jesus. And if God could use Eldred, He can use anybody. The real question isn't "What qualifications do you have?" but "Can you believe?"

My story and Eldred's are polar opposites. I was raised within church walls; Eldred grew up on streets that bore little kindness. We've both had to learn to surrender who we thought we should be so God could shape who we truly are. I've walked along his calling, he along mine—and we've learned neither of us could do it alone.

When Sojourn Church looked to support missions, we didn't start by planning buildings or recruiting committees. We asked, "Who is already in the trenches?" Eldred answered that call—no fanfare. He just showed up and said "Yes." This book is the chronicle of that "yes," and of every life that echoed it back to God.

If you hold this book today, know this: you're not just reading a memoir, you're stepping into a story of resurrection—of broken lives, broken places, and broken hearts made whole. My prayer is that as you turn these pages, you too will hear the call, see the miracles, and say, like Eldred, "Yes, Lord."

–PASTOR TERRY MOORE
Sojourn Church

CHAPTER ONE

Before My Beginning

My first encounter with the power of God didn't come from a man in a three-piece suit standing behind a pulpit. It didn't happen under the glow of stained glass or backed by the hum of a choir. No, sir. It came from a little old lady in a pink bathrobe, fluffy slippers, with curlers in her hair—my grandmother.

I must've been about 10 years old. It was summertime, and we were doing what boys do—lighting off Roman candles in the street, thinking we were invincible. I shot one across the road and dared the neighbor boy to go chase it. He was my age, maybe younger, and without thinking twice, he ran right into the path of an oncoming car.

There was a sickening thud—and I remember how the car didn't stop right away. It dragged him several feet before finally spitting him out onto the pavement out the back of the car. I stood there frozen, the firework still smoking in my hand. That boy lay in the road, dead.

People started gathering. Neighbors came running out, covering their mouths, probably whispering prayers, and staring at the body. I turned and sprinted to their house, yelling through the screen door for his mama. But it wasn't his mother who came first—it was my grandmother.

She came out like a woman on a mission, because she was. She didn't say "excuse me" as she passed through the crowd. She said "MOVE," and people moved. That little woman stormed through the crowd with her slippers slapping the pavement. She dropped to her knee beside the boy, laid one hand on his chest, and prayed without a hint of doubt, "In the name of Jesus ... LIVE!"

Right then, the boy coughed. Air filled his lungs in a deep breath, and his eyes opened wide. He came back and lived to play another day.

Needless to say, his parents weren't too keen on letting him hang out with me after that, but I walked away from that street corner a changed boy. I had witnessed an authentic resurrection. Not in a church service, not in a Bible story—but right there, in the middle of a neighborhood street in Dallas, through the hands of a woman who simply *believed*. And not just some random woman who believed but the woman who would act as a rope, keeping me tethered to the faith through my childhood.

I didn't fully understand it at the time, but something in me shifted. I knew from that moment on that God was real. Not just real—but *active*. Alive. Able. And I would carry that knowledge with me for the rest of my life, no matter how far off track I wandered. Because once you see God move like that, you don't easily forget it.

It was my grandmother—affectionately referred to as Nanny Bishop—whose own salvation changed my bloodline forever.

Before she ever laid hands on the lifeless boy in the street, she'd been laid hold of by something far greater. My grandmother wasn't born into holiness. She came up tough but very gifted. She was a musical prodigy, a performer, and a firecracker of a woman with five marriages behind her before Christ found her. As an actress she played the leading lady in a musical at the legendary Music Hall at Fair Park, but when she got saved, she turned her back on everything but Jesus and never married or performed again. It was a clean break with the old life and a wholehearted immersion into the new one.

My mother, Lorena Austin, was her only child. And while Nanny Bishop passed down her knack for music and flair, the stage gave my mother heartbreak. Mom had been a child star, born in 1921. She was the mayor of Dallas's favorite, dancing and performing in the vaudeville circuits. We have newspaper clippings showing her in spotlight after spotlight—big smiles, bigger dreams. She was even a Hollywood hopeful once. There was talk of a contract—one she never got to sign. Nanny Bishop had just gotten saved in a Pentecostal tent revival and at that time there was no room for show business in the church. They were seen as two separate worlds and my mother's showbiz career came to a halt. The story went that Shirley Temple got the deal that my mother was supposed to sign. That moment marked something in my mom. You could call it the first time she died.

I don't feel she ever really recovered from it, seeing Shirley's career rise like a meteor and her own life spiral. She carried herself like a woman stuck between worlds—too broken for the stage, too bruised for the pew. She tried to build a life, having a marriage and two sons (my half brothers) decades before meeting my father.

The circumstances of my parents' meeting are not known to me. In fact, for most of my life, any detail of my father's history was unknown to me. I was 2 years old when he went to the store in Nanny Bishop's car to get some eggs and we never saw or heard from him again. Needless to say, he was flighty and elusive, even to his own boy. He was a ghost, and for most of my life, I didn't know a thing about him. And I learned early on that a boy who grows up without a father's hand on his shoulder spends half his life looking for the weight of that hand that should've been there all along.

I eventually found out his real name was Calvin Sawyer, born in Edenton, North Carolina, sometime in the 1920s. He'd come to Texas living under a false name. Turns out, he was running from the law. He'd written hot checks across the country and had been living off fraud for years. He and my mother actually pastored a United Pentecostal Church together for some time. Folks said he was a dynamic preacher, and when the truth came out that he'd been using an assumed name, the whole congregation was stunned. He was arrested, sent to prison, and after he served his time, he came back under his real name—and my mother remarried him—having me not long after.

From what I've pieced together over the years, my father was a man of extremes. Raised in North Carolina, he got sent to reform school in his teens. He fought in the Korean War—a bloody, messy, terrible war where he saw plenty of action. Mother said he'd wake up in cold sweats, haunted by night terrors.

A chef by trade, he worked at a country club in Dallas and even ran a little café with my mom for a time. Folks say he was one of the best fry cooks around. It didn't matter how busy the kitchen got, waitresses could holler orders from across the room, and he'd never miss a beat. But behind the sizzle and spice was a man drowning. He'd drink heavy, then go through long spells of sobriety before falling again. After he left us, he became a merchant marine, out on ships, cooking at sea. A man always running—running from his past, from the law, and I believe, from God. And somewhere in the middle of all that running, I was born.

July 30, 1956—Dallas, Texas. I came into the world not with any drama, but with eyes wide open, already trying to figure the place out. I've always thought my name was a little unusual: *Eldred*. Turns out, I was named after the doctor who delivered me. My parents liked the name, which is an Old English word meaning "venerable counsel." Time would tell if I would live up to my name. In the meantime, I was just a little boy—born into the mess of my parents' unraveling story, too young to know what I'd inherited, for better or worse.

* * *

Before I entered this world, there were things already set in motion that would shape my destiny. I was born into a blood-line that carried the gospel—whether we always lived like it or not. My grandmother's conversion lit a fire that still burns in me today. But don't let that fool you. The circumstances weren't perfect. Not even close.

Joseph, in the book of Genesis, comes to mind. He was highly favored, wore a coat of many colors, had a big call-ing—but those things didn't protect him from the pit. His own brothers threw him in a hole, sold him into slavery, and left him for dead. You'd think that kind of betrayal would can-cel the call of God. But instead, every step down was really a step forward in disguise. He went from the pit, to Potiphar's house, to prison—before he ever made it to the palace. And when he got there, it wasn't just about him. God had posi-tioned him to save the very nation and people he came from.

Despite the promise and the call of God that I sensed ear-ly on, I would walk through a few pits and betrayals before seeing it come to pass. I was born into poverty and abandon-ment. My poor mother was unfit in many ways, already a shell of who she once was and a shell of who she could be. By the time I was born, she was almost 40. Depression marked her life, and with that came alcohol and a dependency on prescription meds. She'd stay clean for a season, then crash hard.

I would ride with Nanny Bishop through some of the darkest parts of town, looking for my mom during her binges. We'd find her in beer joints, flop houses, passed out or worse. Nanny Bishop would collect her, give her one beer a day from a six-pack to ease the shakes, get her dried out, and march her right back to church. She knew when to be tender and when to be tough. On one occasion she slapped my PE teacher for leaving welts on me with a paddle—apparently the man said something she didn't much appreciate, and she let him have it. She was a lioness when she needed to be.

I remember her in her long-sleeved flannel gown, her hair tied up in the old Pentecostal bun. Every now and then she'd have me brush it out for her and she'd talk about the Lord and end times. She once told me, "You'll know the end is near when China rises up and computers take over." Now this was the early '60s, mind you, back when computers were the size of small buildings and lived in basement rooms with punch cards and tape reels. But Nanny Bishop saw the future like a woman who'd already read the last page of the Book—because she did.

In those days, my mom was on a welfare check of $138 a month. That's what we had to live on, supplemented by my grandmother's piano lessons. And somehow, Nanny Bishop made it work. She was the real head of the house, even when she wasn't under our roof. She made things happen, especially for me. If I wanted something bad enough, she'd find a way to get it. I'm talking BB guns and a mini-bike . . . things we had no business affording. Nanny Bishop had a way of making life feel fuller than it was. She'd take me to Wyatt's Cafeteria and treat me with love, even if her purse was near empty.

Our setup was patchy. Mom and I had a little 700 square foot rental house, and Nanny Bishop had her own place—but truthfully, Nanny Bishop lived in and out of both, depending on where the need was greatest.

We didn't do vacations; I didn't know what those were. We were dirt poor, but I didn't feel it until school reminded me. Other kids had new clothes while I had rough threads, but Nanny Bishop would scrape together what she could to get me a couple school outfits from Levines. She hustled teaching piano—even had a little home studio—and worked for Brook Mays in downtown Dallas at one point. Her claim was she could teach anyone to play in six weeks, and she made believers out of her students.

Despite the name *Pleasant Grove*, being raised there wasn't always "pleasant." Fist fights, back-porch drinking, folks living on fumes. It was the kind of place that raised scrappers—and I became one. There was a man down the street named Mr. Christmas. Funny name, decent man. He was a sketch artist for the FBI, and for a little while, he showed me attention like a father would. Took me fishing and gave me time. For a moment, I thought maybe he'd stick. But I had a mouth on me. I'd test people, push, and prod. He snapped one day after I had successfully gotten under his skin, and just like that, he was gone too.

Same with my mom's boyfriends. I ran them off like pests. I didn't want another man stepping in. If she brought someone home, I made sure to be on my worst behavior and they learned quickly—it was a package deal and I was not going to be an afterthought in my own house. I could be as mean as I needed to be. At the same time, in my heart of hearts, I was a sweet boy with a gift and no direction. In the midst of all the madness and insecurity, God had planted something in me: I could sing. Even as a child I had a solid voice. My music teacher, Mrs. Taylor, saw something in me, taking me to churches to sing and even buying me clothes for performances. She let me into their home—nice brick place in a clean neighborhood. Sat me at a table where people prayed before meals and used manners, giving me a good taste of functional living.

I sang on TV a few times and got leading roles in school plays. The performance bug that bit my mother and grandmother had gotten into me also. It was more than performance though—there was an anointing on my life. When I sang in churches, I felt the flow of heaven. I vividly recall beginning to see the world in two layers even before the age of ten. I could see what was natural and what was spiritual. I could feel light and darkness wrestling in the room. I remember sitting on my bed and hearing chatter in the spirit that nobody else heard, like a fight between godly and sinister voices. I heard God affirming me with things like, "Do what is right. I'll always be with you." I knew it was Him, clear as day. Since the moment I gave my heart to the Lord as a child at the altar of the UPC church, I had a heart for God. Prophecies flowed into my life from folks at our local congregation. The truth is, people saw a calling on me even back then. I'd say things wise beyond my years and carried a kind of *knowing* I couldn't explain. I've even got a photo of me from when I was 2 years old—Bible in one hand, finger pointed up and out, like I was already preaching.

I was a sweet boy, but I learned to survive in a rough world. I successfully hid my tears from my mama. Wedging myself between the bed and the wall, face pressed into the mattress, I would cry, "Why didn't my daddy love me?

Why did he leave?" But I never let her hear me in the other room. That pain eventually hardened into anger. And that father wound was the beginning of my descent into the life I'd eventually need saving from.

Before he left, my dad gave me the nickname *Hardrock*. Apparently it was because I'd fall and smack my head on the coffee table while learning to walk and then get back up without shedding a tear. I hated that name, not because of the name itself but because of the man who gave it to me. If he could not stay for me, he hadn't earned the right to name me. Nevertheless, hardness became a core theme of my childhood.

I saw and experienced things very early on that would be worthy now of the words *trauma* or *abuse*. As young as age 4, I had been exposed and forced into sexual activity with a girl who was baby sitting me. She was a late teenager at the time. It was not a one-off event but became a spiritual pattern that stuck in my life. By age 7 or 8, I had lost my virginity to a teenage girl down the street, and this pattern awakened a template in me that would become a battle in the long run.

Innocence didn't have a long lease on my life. At the time I didn't even understand what was being stolen from me. It planted thoughts in me I had no business wrestling with as a child. The abuse was a kind of spiritual robbery—and the enemy loves to strike early, to scar you young so you limp through life never realizing you were born to run.

I developed emotional callouses when a lot of kids were just figuring out how to tie their shoes and swing a baseball bat. Beyond my own household, relatives weren't exactly handing out tenderness either, having no extended family, and the half brothers were busy raising families of their own. Kindness wasn't common. In Pleasant Grove, gentleness was something you had to squint to find. One memory sticks sharp—I had a puppy that got really sick. I must have been just 6 years old at the time. I brought it to my half brother Austin, a man two decades older than me, hoping he'd help. Instead, he took the pup, laid it on the concrete, and swung a ball-peen hammer at its head, killing it on the spot. He said it was better that way, it would have died slowly anyway. Perhaps that was the case, but the idea of shielding a six-year-old from that sight hadn't occurred to him. Another brick in the wall of my callousness was added.

Here's the redemptive reminder: destiny doesn't need perfect soil. It can grow in the dark. It can grow in dysfunction. God never waits on ideal conditions to start His plan. Just like Joseph—sold out, locked up, forgotten—yet God raised him up to lead nations. I didn't know it then, but God was setting something in motion in my life, too. If He could raise Joseph up from betrayal and prison, He could raise up a preacher from the hard streets of Dallas.

CHAPTER TWO

When the Anchor Breaks

The smell of burnt toast changed my life.

It was a small thing, but on that day, it marked the start of the biggest shift I had ever known. Breakfast burning signaled to me that the bottom started falling out of my world.

I was 12 years old. Nanny Bishop had come to wake me for school like she always did. I asked if I could stay in bed a few extra minutes while she got breakfast going, and she smiled and said, "Alright." She would wake me when she had a plate ready.

But then I woke again—not to Nanny Bishop's voice, but to the smell of burnt butter and charred toast on the cast iron skillet. I stumbled out to the kitchen, still rubbing sleep from my eyes.

She was on the floor.

Her eyes were open, and she was breathing, but something was wrong. She couldn't speak, but I knew she could hear me. She responded with her eyes, even nodded when I talked. I remember a strange calm washing over me, like I had stepped out of panic and into purpose. I've had moments like that throughout my life—crisis hitting and the Spirit steadying me along the way.

My mother came in and lost it in a hysterical fit of screaming and crying. But I knelt down beside Nanny Bishop and whispered, "Nanny, I know you can't talk. But can you let Mama know you're okay with a smile?"

And she did—just the gentlest, faintest smile.

The ambulance came fast, but it didn't matter. Nanny Bishop was gone before we ever got to the hospital. She was 72 years old.

The moment she died, I felt something spiritual hit me. Like a robe being laid across my shoulders. The comfort of her responsibility, her prayer covering—it was gone. And I knew deep down, it was all on me now. I was just a kid, but I knew I was the man of the house and totally responsible for my mother and myself from that day forward.

At my grandmother's funeral, I ran out of the familiar UPC church, mad as ever at God. I didn't care who saw it.

Didn't care who understood. The only person who ever made me feel stable was in a box, and I was done trying.

That's exactly when the spiral began.

I turned to drinking, drugs, weed—anything to fill the gaping hole that had been left in her place. By 15, I had a needle in my arm. You don't fall that fast unless there was already something cracked underneath. I knew God was real. I'd seen miracles. But when she died, I didn't know how to reconcile His power with my pain.

Perhaps that whole stretch—from age 12 to 30—wasn't just rebellion. Maybe it was my wilderness. Like the Israelites, wandering 40 years before ever touching the promise. Like Jesus, baptized and called "Beloved," only to be led straight into the desert. Formation can feel like destruction when you're still in it. The Bible says, "And you shall remember that the LORD your God led you all the way these forty years in the wilderness, to humble you and test you, to know what was in your heart, whether you would keep His commandments or not" (Deuteronomy 8:2).

But before I take you deeper into that brokenness, let me say this: We don't revisit pain to glorify it. We revisit pain to understand redemption. God doesn't hide the scars of His people—He highlights them. David's adultery. Moses's murder. Peter's denial. The Word of God doesn't skip over the mess, and neither should we, because it's the pit that makes the rescue so powerful.

So as we walk through a darker chapter of my life, don't mistake transparency for pride. I'm not telling you these things to shock you or to celebrate sin—in fact, there's plenty that I've left out. I'm writing these things so you can see how far grace can reach. Because the truth is, after Nanny Bishop died, I came apart at the seams. I was 12, full of pain, and had no grid for how to live life. That's when the anger kicked in full force—and I didn't even know yet that anger is just hurt wearing a harder face.

Until then I had always been well liked in school, believe it or not. I was funny, sharp, and made great marks. But I was restless. Probably undiagnosed ADHD or something approximating it. I couldn't sit still; academic focus was torture. If I figured out a teacher had a nerve, I'd spend every class trying to push on it. There was something about getting a rise out of people that made me feel in control. Antagonism became a form of entertainment. Eventually I started skipping class more than I'd show up. The wheels had already come off my life, why bother sitting in front of a chalkboard? I coasted on common sense and street smarts, but I wasn't building a future.

By the time I was in my early teens, I had illusions of

grandeur about becoming some kind of drug kingpin. In my head, I'd be rich, respected, untouchable. But that was just the broken boy in me trying to rewrite the script he'd been handed.

And then came the rage.

I remember the first time I really snapped. I was 13. There was this older kid—cool, tough, always surrounded by girls. He let me hang around but made sure I knew my place. He'd pop me in the arm, frog me in front of his buddies, belittle me just enough to keep me angry but silent. One day at his house, he pulled out a bullwhip—started showing off, popping it near me, laughing. I kept telling him to cut it out. He didn't. Finally, he ran me down a hallway, and when I hit the dead end, something inside me broke. I turned, snatched that whip out of his hands, and beat him senseless with the wooden handle, leaving him bruised and bloodied.

And just like that, I found a feeling that I savored—power. I made a silent vow: Hurt them before they hurt you. That became a philosophy, a defense, but in reality *a sickness*. And I carried it with me like a weapon. I surprised myself with rage more times than I can count, and that ultimately became a decades-long battle. Looking back, it's a miracle of God that I didn't end up with a murder charge to my name.

School didn't last much longer. It was an era of racial integration, and tensions were high in the school system. I had nothing whatsoever against the new black students, though some of them felt a right to antagonize at times. On one particular day, a black kid walked up to me and demanded, "Gimme a quarter."

I calmly said, "I don't have a quarter for you," and he popped me on the jaw in response. As you can imagine, I didn't tuck my tail and run like a whipped puppy. I splattered his nose in short order, and the next thing I knew, I was jumped by all his friends like a swarm of bees. My white buddies? They all took off running.

I never went back to school for a single day after that. My schooling ended in a physical dispute, not a diploma. That was in the ninth grade.

From that moment on, I was out of school and out of bounds. No teachers, no schedules, no discipline. Just loose ends and open roads. I was 15 with no limits. It was the early 1970s in Pleasant Grove, Texas, and the whole world felt like it was running wild with me. Southern rock was the soundtrack—long hair, dope, rebellion. There were hints of "hippie freedom" in the air, but we weren't the pacifist types, to say the least.

And all the while, I was trying to hold together what little family I had left.

Nanny Bishop was gone, mother was broken, and I was still doing what I'd learned as a kid—dragging her out of bars and binges, trying to keep her somewhat safe. But this time, there was no one left to back me up. I was a kid, trying to play the part of a grown man in a broken home.

Despite me often caring for her, my mom did her best to look out for me, as well. As I came into my teenage years, she saw I was slipping fast. And she knew I needed more than hugs and hope. That's when she called in Austin. Austin and Crayton were my two older half brothers. They were about 20 years older than me and a year apart. Crayton took more after my mother—rough around the edges and deep in addiction.

Austin, on the other hand, was cut from a different cloth. He was tough, no-nonsense. Had a short fuse and was a true rage-aholic. But he built a business from nothing as a home builder and hard worker. He had actually been a youth pastor once, but got caught up in scandal, had an affair, and walked away from the church. Still, deep down, he loved the Lord. I'd catch him crying to old gospel tapes, headphones on, but he never went back to church. He was a man split in half—one side still reaching for God, the other too proud to turn back.

I was 15 when Austin was looped in to straighten me out.

I moved into a spare room at his house. While on the drive to his house, he told me plain and simple, "Monday morning, you're coming to work with me."

That sounded okay with me. He then asked, "What do you want out of life?"

Sarcastically, I shot back, "A motorcycle."

He looked at me hard. "Your mama's always told you you're just a poor little boy whose daddy left, deserving sympathy. But nobody cares. That attitude ain't gonna get you anywhere. Nobody owes you anything. Monday morning— you work."

And just like that, my lazy summer plans were cancelled.

Truth is, my mother *would* make excuses for me and made a victim out of me fairly often. Austin made no room for that. He too had a father who had abandoned him and took off to LA, made a bunch of money, and never reached out to him or Crayton. He knew my pain and also knew that I wouldn't succeed if I allowed that pain to bury me in a victim mentality.

Austin meant business. He told me he'd flip on the light every morning at 5 a.m., then go brush his teeth—and if I wasn't up by the time he was done, he'd drag me out of bed by my hair. That first morning, the light flipped on and I stayed in bed. About ten minutes later, I was, in fact, being dragged out of bed by my hair.

Every morning after that, I jumped out of bed before that toothbrush was in his hand. We would head off to the job site and he worked me like a grown man. Hot Texas summer, framing houses, raw hands, splinters, and sunburnt skin. If he caught you trying to dig out a splinter or tend to a blister, what he'd say was always the same: "Draw a circle around it, and deal with it on your time. You're on my clock." Friday came, and payday hit. Austin stood in front of the worn down crew and handed out checks. One by one everybody got a check but me.

"Where's mine?" I asked.

"Boy, you ain't worth what it costs to feed you and house you."

That stung. But I had no choice. This went on all summer. No pay, no praise. Just sweat and sore muscles.

That summer under Austin's roof wasn't just about learning how to work—it was about learning how to take a hit and keep moving. If I hit my thumb with my hammer, or stepped on a nail, Austin would look at me and say, "It'll feel better when it quits hurtin'. Let's go."

He tried to do right by me, in his own hard way. But his brand of discipline came from distance, not relationship. He didn't know how to be gentle with a broken kid. He just knew how to enforce order. And that too had its perfect work.

One time, he thought I was stealing his cigarettes. Turned out, it was someone else all along. But he didn't ask questions—he just brought me in and whipped me. I made up my mind I wasn't going to cry, no matter what. He kept shouting, "You gonna cry, boy?" I just stared at him stone cold, mad, and silent. My mom was visiting that day and stepped in eventually, crying and begging him to stop, and he did. Needless to say, it was not a perfect mentorship and we butted heads often. Later on, I stood up to him in a way that surprised even me. He was a tough sucker to fight, and by the time the police showed up, I was quite happy to see them.

Austin was a passionate man—he loved deeply, but he didn't know how to show it. Everything with him came out strong. He once told me he should've been born in Missouri—"It's the Show-Me State," he said, "and I gotta be shown." That was Austin. Words didn't move him, proof did.

Despite the craziness, that summer taught me more than any classroom ever could. I learned how to show up, sweat, and push through. I learned that excuses don't build houses—and neither do free handouts. I hated it while I was in it, but looking back, I can see it laid the foundation for something I'd carry for the rest of my life.

The cherry on top of the whole ordeal was driving home on the last day of summer with Austin. I noticed he took a detour and pulled into a Suzuki shop. On the spot he bought me a 90cc Enduro street legal dirt bike. No doubt, he had planned it for me but kept silent about it all summer. That dirt bike was his way of saying, "I see you. I love you."

What he actually said was a short and sweet reminder: "That's what you get when you work."

It was the first real lesson in manhood I ever got—you don't get what you want for nothing. You earn it. I told him I wanted a motorcycle out of life, and I had the keys for it a few months later.

After my stint with Austin, I moved back home with my mom. By then, Crayton had been through a divorce and was living there too, along with his four children. He was soft-spoken when sober, a mess when he wasn't. I loved him, but he was broken—and so was I.

Together, we turned that rental house into a party house.

Drugs, booze, chaos—everything Nanny Bishop would've shut down in a heartbeat, we welcomed in like family. My mother was doing her best to keep it together, but we were tearing the place apart. She was on the verge of losing her mind, and looking back, I don't blame her.

I had used intravenously for the first time while living with Austin at 15 and then went off the rails after moving back with my mom at 16. Too young to legally drive a car and shooting up. It wasn't exactly your average coming-of-age story. Crayton and I were codependent—two broken guys feeding off each other's destruction. Growing up in a UPC church, they preached hard on the return of Jesus. I remember occasionally looking up in the mornings after an all-nighter on speed, staring at the cloudy Texas skies, wondering, *Is this the day? Will the sky crack open? And if it does, where does that leave me?*

Nevertheless, my fearful pondering did not stop the addiction.

By the time I was 16, I reached a place where I'd been up for 28 straight days on meth. No sleep. Little food. Just this manic, wild-eyed buzz that wouldn't quit. The visions I was having weren't just drug-induced hallucinations, they felt spiritual. Dark, chaotic, supernatural. The Bible uses the word *pharmakeia* for witchcraft, which is where we get our word *pharmacy*. I believe there's a dark link between drugs and the supernatural that's seldom discussed. Drugs don't just numb you, they open doors. And I had opened too many, too young.

They finally sent me to the state mental hospital in Terrell, Texas. I landed in the adolescent ward—what passed for a rehab back in the early '70s. Hippies, junkies, and kids spun out on acid and speed. It was a holding tank for the lost.

I sat with a counselor in that place. I was hollow, angry, strung out, and searching for anything that would tell me who I was. And they gave me something: "Borderline Antisocial Personality Disorder."

Now, for some people, that might've been a warning. For me, it was a label I latched onto. I didn't have a name that carried meaning. I was the only Sawyer in my family. My daddy had disappeared, I knew no one on my father's side, and I was grasping for identity. So when they handed me that diagnosis, it didn't scare me, it defined me.

I looked up the symptoms years later, and it fit. Calloused. No remorse, empathy, or real feeling. You don't just wake up like that. You get shaped into it. And I was halfway down the path to becoming a sociopath—and too numb to care.

* * *

People talk about the good, the bad, and the ugly when they tell their story. During this stretch of my life, it was just bad and ugly. There wasn't a silver lining or a lesson in real time. It was addiction, heartbreak, betrayal, jail, and a slow descent into spiritual ruin. But I've learned something about the Lord in retrospect: He doesn't run from rock bottom, He meets us there.

In Mark 5 we see a story about a man so far gone, he lived

in a graveyard. Full of demons, covered in scars from self-cutting, he was chained up and screaming at the sky. Folks had written him off. He was too dangerous to fuss with. But Jesus crossed a stormy sea just to get to him and restore him.

I like to think that when my life went from bad to worse, and that season had its perfect work, God rubbed His hands together and said, "Now it's My turn."

And things certainly did go from bad to worse. After my brief stint in the mental institution, sobriety didn't last long. I dried out for a bit, but as my late teen years rolled in, I was right back in the thick of it. As they say, I was busted, disgusted, and couldn't be trusted. Addiction became the oxygen I breathed, and I began to lose everything that meant anything to me. Slowly at first, then all at once.

At 17, I met ValJean. She was just 15, already had a daughter not yet two. Pregnant at 12 and a mother at 13. Her world was darker than mine. Her mama was a heroin addict, a booster—shoplifting was her trade—and she raised Val in that lifestyle. Instead of school, Val would create diversions in the store while her mother filled her pockets and purse. By 12, Val had already had her first hit of heroin, courtesy of her own mother. By 14, her habit became too expensive and her mom dropped her off at a pimp's place.

Val was raised as a child in a home with nine different

cousins and a brother, children who all had been raised primarily by their grandma. Most of the criminal, addicted parents were either gone or in jail. Something in Val's family felt familiar. Her cousins, brothers, friends—they accepted me. And I, a young man with no family tree, no Sawyer lineage behind me, felt like I'd finally been claimed. I had known some of Val's siblings from school and there was almost a mob-like sense of having each other's back. They were tough and feared in the streets.

Before long, Val and I moved in together in an apartment I rented—and my mom moved in, as well. Not only did I immediately become a stepdad, but we started having kids of our own quickly. It was dysfunction in the purest form. We were kids raising kids—addicted and trying to play house. Val and I had two children together in a couple year span, a boy and a girl. When I looked into the faces of my children, I felt something I couldn't shake: awe and wonder. In my heart of hearts, I wanted to be a father—and a good one. Even in the throes of my addiction, I wanted to be everything I lacked growing up.

I made vows early on, telling myself I'd never be like my sorry dad. But in reality, I probably became worse. I had zero grid for what a good father looked like and no concept of biblical fatherhood. By the time the state stepped in, we were strung out, sleeping in cars. We had two children of our own, plus Val's daughter. We'd get a little better for a season, but nothing stuck—addiction ate every good intention. I would work for Austin here and there but could not maintain a job. Eventually, onlookers reported us to CPS (Child Protective Services), and the kids were taken into foster care.

That crushed me instantly. I had known the pain of a father being removed from my life and was now walking through the pain of my children being removed from my life—and because of my own failures, no less. We wanted our kids back and quickly began making a plan to right our wrongs. Val and I went to church and remained sober. We listened to the preachers and even got married in the church. In truth we were trying to play God like a fiddle. No true repentance, just sorry for our mess and hoping we could manipulate God to fix it. If we just got our acts together, we'd get our kids back and life would be peachy.

For a year and a half, we did everything the state required: sobriety, rehab, parenting classes, steady jobs. Eighteen months of trying to prove we were fit. We had done the required programs, and I was holding down steady work. We had a guardian ad litem assigned to the kids, and we thought we were making headway.

Then I got a letter—there was an upcoming hearing.

I called our court-appointed representative. "Where do we meet?"

"You don't need to go. You should work. It's a formality. I'll represent you."

Three weeks later, we got another letter: our parental rights had been terminated.

Why? Because we didn't show up to the hearing. We found out later that the woman representing us was dating the guy in the court who was prosecuting us. Needless to say, she gave us bad information. We didn't even find out there was a ten-day appeal window after that error until a year later.

I was devastated. Mad at God, mad at people—but the truth is, I hadn't been walking with Him. I was using Him. Even during that clean year and a half, God was a means to an end, not an end in Himself. I wasn't surrendered or submitted, I was bargaining.

By then, the gloves were off. We were back so deep in the spiral of addiction, it felt like there was no turning back. I was reaching the lowest of lows both in my drug use and also in my rage. With the direction I was heading, if the drugs didn't take me out, some murder charge probably would—or one of the people I was bullying or taking advantage of would've killed me first. I had a very calculated and patient rage. If you had crossed a line, I would wait my turn, but eventually, I would get you. These are not things I boast in but things I *confess*—because they show just how far gone I was, and how far grace had to reach to find me.

On one occasion, a guy had borrowed money from my mother's welfare check. She wasn't a bank so I didn't like the idea to begin with, but as collateral he left her with a suede jacket. A month or two went by and he didn't pay her, so she retained the collateral and gave me the jacket. He went to get it from her, she explained herself, and in response he cussed her out and made serious threats.

I let it lay for a long time.

I was not a reactionary rage-aholic but a calm one. I invited the guy over under the guise of giving him dope and brought him into the bathroom where I locked the door and beat him mercilessly. He was pretty much unconscious when I held him under hot water in the tub trying to drown him. The other guy in the apartment broke the door down to pull me off of him. Thank God!

Between rage fits and dealer visits, life didn't stop. It just got heavier. Val and I had two more kids after that—Lonnie and Meredith. But addiction followed us. During that season, Val caught a 25-year prison sentence on a robbery charge, and I was dragging our two kids through hell.

And somewhere in that season came another hit.

At the age of 62, my mama died. Her body had been worn down by years of depression and pills. She didn't drink as much toward the end, but the damage had been done. She had a massive stroke, and when I saw her before she passed, she was frail—drawn up, one leg tucked under her chin like a shell of herself. She didn't want to be seen that way.

So many of the folks I had loved and known were dying, on the run, or being incarcerated. While Val was behind bars, I also caught a possession case. From jail, Val made an attempt to protect the kids from me. She knew I was falling fast, knew it wouldn't be long before I got arrested again or worse. From prison, she contacted Buckner's Orphan Home, trying to line up care for Lonnie and Meredith.

In short order, a man from Buckner's came out, trying to get me to sign the kids over, warning that if I didn't, he would bring CPS into the picture. At the time I was living in an apartment with a bonafide psychopath named Deadeye—who was one of Val's cousins and came from the shady childhood home they all grew up in—and my two kids. Lonnie was 3 and Meredith was 6. I told Deadeye, "If that man comes back out to try to take the kids, I'll kill him and put him in the lake."

And I meant every word.

To compound the chaos, Deadeye and I were planning a robbery at the time. The apartment complex we lived in was entirely a criminal enterprise. The management, security, maintenance—it was all a front for prostitution, drug dealing, gambling. A man would come in with a brief case on Fridays and charge a 20% fee to cash paychecks for illegals. The briefcase had somewhere around $80,000 to $100,000 inside and two armed guards stood at each end of the table. The plan? Shoot our way in, take the cash, and shoot our way out.

I had no sense of what I was doing to those kids, or to my own soul, but I was not off God's radar. He was watching the whole mess and making plans to frustrate my own. In the next few days, I was headed for one of three endings: put someone in a body bag, end up in one myself, or have God tear it all down and build something new from the wreckage I had created.

I had already lost three of my kids and I was about to lose two more. As the only one left standing with Lonnie and Meredith, I knew I probably wouldn't be standing for long. Addiction had me by the throat, the system was knocking at the door, and I could feel the walls closing in.

CHAPTER THREE

Running at the Barking Dog

I woke up on the morning of the robbery in our messy apartment. The TV had been left on all night with the volume turned down. When I opened my eyes, there was a preacher on the screen. I couldn't tell you who he was or what he was saying, but there he stood behind the pulpit, preaching the Word of God.

From somewhere outside of myself, I was hit with an immediate realization that I *had* to get up and do something right then. The knowing came with extreme urgency, like a last warning. I knew if something didn't change, I'd go through with that robbery, I'd kill the man from the orphanage, I would quite possibly die at some point in the process, and I could for sure be saying goodbye to my kids once and for all. The urgency was like dashing to the last boarding call on a flight you're about to miss—but multiplied by a million. The Holy Spirit quickened me with a jolt that I could not shake. I knew it in my bones: "You've got to do something right now."

I got up, ran to a pay phone, and dialed the one Christian that I knew: Allen Gernhardt, the pastor where we attended while trying to play God the last time. I told him my situation and he said, "I can't come to get you right now. I've got a house full of missionaries staying with me. But I'll give you the number of a man who can help."

I scribbled down the number—and that number became a seven-digit bridge to the purpose I would pursue for the rest of my life.

After dialing, a man named Leonard Brannon picked up.

I wasted no time telling him I needed help. It wasn't dramatic. It wasn't polished. But it was urgent. And somehow, I knew it was a kairos moment, a God-timed turning point, though I didn't have the language for it at the time.

Not wanting to get rejected, I almost tried to talk Leonard out of helping me. I said, "Listen, I'm a criminal and a heroin addict. I need $1,000 a day to support my habit. I'm probably going to jail because I've got felony warrants on me right now—"

"Where are you?" he said, cutting me off.

I told him my location before I could finish trying to scare him away. He wasn't bothered in the slightest, either naivety or love. Nonetheless he said with conviction, "I'm gonna send someone to get you right now."

I was 30 years old and on my way to a new life I didn't see coming.

The guy Leonard sent to pick me up wasn't a preacher, wasn't a counselor—just a guy who was staying in Leonard's home. But he showed up, and that was more than many people had done for me.

I didn't know much about the man on the other end of the line that day—Leonard Brannon—but I would come to learn that he was on a mission of his own. At that time, Leonard was just getting started in carrying out the vision that was in his heart. He'd been a church kid—what I might've called a square back then—but he had been gripped with a vision to start a ministry and to care for the poor, the addicted, the disenfranchised, and I fit the bill to a tee. In July of 1986, he and an old high school friend rented a storage unit and started stockpiling food to feed the homeless. Just cans and boxes at first, but it was vision in seed form.

By October of that year, he'd filed the paperwork and officially launched CareCenter Ministries. Between then and

January 1987, he'd taken in a few guys off the street. I was the third. He had made a decision to forsake all, leave his secular job, and move derelicts like myself into his home with his wife and children. He was either crazy or truly called.

When I walked into Leonard's home, I thought I was walking into a temporary fix—a place to get sober, stay out of jail, maybe hang onto my kids for another week or two. My motivations were mixed: I was responding to the urgent call to *get up and do something* and I was also wanting to keep my two children under my care.

I had no idea I was walking into destiny.

Within that first week, by God's grace, I had found true repentance. I knew somehow: My life wasn't my own anymore. I wasn't just saved, I was arrested by grace. I was a prisoner of the Lord, and I knew I was never going back to normal life according to this world's systems. The move to Leonard's home was like a dying plant being taken to a new pot with fresh soil, water, and sunlight. It marked the start of my transformation.

Because my atmosphere changed, my appetites changed. I didn't just stop using drugs, I stopped craving the life that came with them. The fog began to lift. My thoughts weren't racing, my hands weren't shaking, and for the first time in years, I could sit in silence without being swallowed by it.

I was starting to *feel* again. For years, I'd been numb, diagnosed antisocial, wrapped in layers of callousness that protected me from pain but kept out everything else too. Now, little by little, those layers were peeling off, and a heart for others was coming alive in me.

Cleaning up your life brings some pain and suffering, sure, but it also brings clarity. And in that clarity, I started seeing who I really was. Not just what I'd done wrong, but what I let myself become and what God by His abundant mercy and grace might still make out of me.

"Now I rejoice, not that you were made sorry, but that your sorrow led to repentance. For you were made sorry in a godly manner, that you might suffer loss from us in nothing. For godly sorrow produces repentance leading to salvation, not to be regretted; but the sorrow of the world produces death." (2 Corinthians 7:9–10)

I started waking up early. Reading Scripture. Praying, even when I didn't feel like it. There was a strength entering me, one decision at a time. I didn't need a platform, I needed purpose.

Before, my goal had been survival—just stay high enough to not feel, just hustle enough to not starve. But now? I wanted to be a man of God. I wanted to be a good father and a voice in dark places.

Getting clean wasn't just about ditching the needle, it was about laying down the identity that had wrapped around my soul like chains. I was getting sober in my body and in my mind, and with every passing day, it felt like my spirit was waking up too.

It was clear: I wasn't going back, not just because I didn't want to, but because God wasn't going to let me. I felt like the rebel Saul who was knocked down on the road, blinded by Jesus, and simply told, "Arise and go into the city, and you will be told what you must do" (Acts 9:6).

Getting plugged in at Leonard's house also meant getting plugged in at his spiritual house, which was Church on the Rock, pastored by Dr. Larry Lea. I had never seen anything like the place. Thousands upon thousands of people would congregate on Sunday mornings and the presence of God was so thick in that church many would walk through the doors and hit their knees. You didn't have to explain your sin, God just read your mail and met you there. Folks would be weeping before the first song ended. It was electric in those days. By then Pastor Larry had written the bestseller *Could You Not Tarry One Hour?* and was preaching on TV every morning at 6 a.m. He'd mobilized 300,000 prayer warriors across the nation, and the prayer meetings were unlike anything I've seen since—1,500 people at 6 a.m. in the church facility in Rockwall, crying out to God for an hour, and then driving back to Dallas for work.

Folks were selling homes, quitting jobs, moving from other states—just to be near what God was doing.

This was the soil I started in.

Spiritual encounters opened up for me quickly. I had a full-on open vision one morning during worship—Jesus standing there, arms open, a smile on His face, and nail holes still in His hands. It wasn't judgment in His eyes. It was an invitation—a new vision for my life. He wasn't just calling me out of darkness, He was calling me into purpose.

I found my footing fast and got my preach on early. My growth was expedited for a couple of reasons. First, I was immersed in this new lifestyle completely and totally from day one. Second, it was not my first run-in with the faith. I had encountered God in my childhood, so in many ways, this new season felt like a homecoming. In fact, I've often wrestled with the question: When was I saved? Most people would probably believe I was saved at 30. Yet I believe I very well could have been authentically saved during that encounter at 9 years old in the UPC church. Then, all the junk that played out until my apprehension at age 30 was part of the wilderness process.

Whether I was born again at 9 or at 30, or both—it happened, and God was upending my life in all the best ways. I was stretched, pressed, grown, challenged, developed, and made to die. Why? So that resurrection power could come.

Within a few weeks, Leonard told me he couldn't keep Lonnie and Meredith in the house full-time, so church families stepped in to help, and I had to face a serious weakness for me: trusting people. I didn't just have trust issues, I had a PhD in not letting folks get too close. In the past I had left my kids with people and later found out they hadn't been fed or cared for properly. I'd physically hurt people over stuff like that. Now that I was in the church and my children were with other families, I heard reports about my kids that would've likely triggered that violent aggression—and I had to learn how to pause, pray, and collect myself before I allowed myself to retaliate. Ultimately, I was learning how to trust God with what I could not control. And be grateful for circumstances out of my control.

It wasn't just spiritual but practical. One night, Leonard had a room full of people—maybe 20 or so who all gathered for a Bible study and dinner. In the middle of it, he turned to me and said, "You got the dishes."

I was hot. Growing up, my mother had put a stray idea into my head that men do *not* do dishes.

As I rolled up my sleeves and got to work in the kitchen, I fumed with that thought that men *don't do dishes*. As I looked down in the middle of scrubbing, I saw a Rolex watch sitting by the sink (I later found out it was a fake). I glanced down at it and saw the back door was wide open and instantly thought, I could drop the dishes, pocket that thing, and slip out. But something broke in me that night. I stayed and scrubbed every plate, every cup, every fork. And for me, that was the start of learning humility, submission, and servanthood that transcends any silly rule or prideful false identity I might have had.

For folks who come out of an absolute mess of a life, they begin learning these spiritual truths and seeing personal breakthroughs quickly—if they'll yield. When you've been scraping rock bottom and God suddenly gives you solid ground, you start running fast. But here's what a lot of people don't talk about: Even when your soul gets right, you still have to deal with the trail you left behind. You might be born again, but your criminal record isn't. You've still got court dates, fines, reputation trouble. Salvation is instant—but cleanup can take time. That's exactly where I found myself in those early years.

I was supposed to serve four years in prison on a probation violation from that possession charge. That was the plan on paper—warrants active, sentencing lined up, children adequately placed with church family, I turned myself in. Before I did, we went to meet with Paul Ecker at Teen Challenge, and something unexpected happened. Paul was old-school tough, the kind of guy you didn't bring excuses to. He could sniff out manipulation before you even opened your mouth. But that day, by nothing short of a miracle, I walked out as though admitted in the program. Technically, I was taking in all of the truths that Teen Challenge would offer, but doing so outside of the physical grounds of the program itself. Not long after, at my court hearing, the judge looked at my status, the program, the changes, and reinstated my probation. Zero jail time required. They made me an outpatient at Teen Challenge and released me back to the ministry. I never even started the program but enjoyed the benefits of being admitted. Paul told me straight, "You're on fire, you and Leonard are building something, and we're going to let you go do it."

It was hard to believe. I knew what I deserved, and it wasn't *that* kind of favor. But God had His hand on it and that meeting opened the door to a freedom that no man could've manufactured.

I'd been walking a line with my probation officer, Mr. Rufus Johnson, for years by then. Even as we moved around—starting the men's home, expanding outreach—he never transferred me. "You make me look good," he'd say, half-smiling. He was fair, but firm. Anytime I got behind on payments, due to having zero income at the time, he'd give me the same line: "You gotta pay your probation fees or they'll take you in."

And I'd answer him just as directly. "Mr. Johnson, I respect your position. You've got a job to do. But so do I. I'm doing what the Lord's told me to do, and if locking me up is what you've got to do, I'll walk in clean and won't run."

That kind of back-and-forth went on for four years. But eventually, the favor wore thin. Rufus called me one day and said, "Eldred, your file is going back to the judge. You're behind $2,500 in probation fees. Once it hits his desk, you're going to jail. I can't keep it off his radar anymore."

I told him the same thing I'd always said, only with a little more weight behind it this time. "I understand. I'm not running. I'll submit if that's what it comes to."

That call happened in the middle of the week. That Sunday, I was in church, standing in the foyer before services. From across the room, I noticed a man I didn't know staring me down. He was locked in, like he had something burning in his chest. He made his way over to me and, without much of a word, slipped a check into my shirt pocket.

He looked me square in the eye and said, "God won't leave me alone about this. I've got to obey Him and give you this."

I pulled out the check: $2,700. He didn't even know my name, leaving the payee blank.

Yes, I needed $2,500 for probation, but I also needed a few items for the kids, and this exact number gave me everything I needed to cover probation and their needs. Down to the dollar, that check took care of it all.

When I told Rufus Johnson, he just about lost his mind. He shouted all over the probation office. Years of watching this walk unfold—watching the change, the consistency, the fruit of our ministry, and the hand of God—and now a miracle check to settle the accounts with the courts. He was charged up, to say the least.

I was off of paper entirely and experiencing new levels of freedom inside and out. There were still challenges galore in those early days, but I wasn't walking through them alone anymore. I had my new church family.

The book of Psalms promises, "God sets the solitary in families; He brings out those who are bound into prosperity; but the rebellious dwell in a dry land" (Psalm 68:6). This passage had become a reality for me.

For the first time in my adult life, I had a clear head, a sense of vision, the Spirit of God, and people who cared, guiding each step. I wasn't just getting by but getting ahead— being transformed, one obedient choice at a time. And as I kept showing up, God kept showing off.

* * *

I knew I was part of something bigger than I could ever build with my own two hands. The biblical concepts of relationships, impartation, honor, submission to authority, and covering had all been impressed on me early on in my walk. In the world, I could be a lone wolf. In the body of Christ, lone wolves had no place.

I had been at the home with Leonard for just six weeks—we didn't even have the men's home up and running yet. Just a small, dusty storefront we were using for a food pantry, running on prayer and a handshake from a landlord too gracious to press us for rent. We were scraping by—me, Leonard, and a young lady helping us form what would become CareCenter Ministries. We didn't have much, but what we did have, God was breathing on.

We were still tied to Church on the Rock through our attendance at the time, but not in any official way. There was no budget, but we had fruit that couldn't be faked. We stayed rooted in prayer. In the early mornings, just a handful of us would gather and cry out to the Lord. During one of those sessions, in the middle of prayer, God spoke to me clear as day:

"You're going to go to New York City to meet David Wilkerson."

After we prayed, I relayed what God had said out loud—I couldn't keep it in. The word was as real to me as the people standing in the room with me.

Nevertheless, a couple people in the room proceeded to laugh out loud at that notion.

I can't blame them. We didn't have a dime to spare, no plans, no connections. How would I go to meet the man who wrote the famous *The Cross and the Switchblade*?

It sounded crazy, but I knew it was God.

Later that same day, I got a phone call from a guy in our Overcomer's group in Rockwall named Greg Isbell. At the time he was helping serve at the Church on the Rock campus down in Duncanville. He said, "This is going to sound strange, but . . . do you have somewhere you're supposed to go?"

I said, "Matter of fact, yeah. The Lord told me this morning I'm supposed to go to New York City to meet David Wilkerson."

He went quiet for a second, then said, "I was talking to Steve Mallow this morning. He's feeling led to fund a trip for someone. When I prayed about it . . . I thought of you."

Steve Mallow was something else. A wealthy guy, clean off addiction, designing clothes for Hollywood types—John Travolta and the like. He didn't just fund the trip. He came along and bought me new clothes, booked a five-star hotel, fed me at top of the line restaurants.

I walked into Times Square Church, across from Port Authority at the time, heart pounding in my chest. I told the ushers where I was from, that I was with a street ministry out of Church on the Rock, and that God had given me a word to come meet David Wilkerson.

They told Pastor David and he invited me backstage. I'm going to take a wild guess and assume that he did not normally do impromptu meetings with no-name folks who come into church asking to meet with him. Nevertheless, God was involved and, the next thing I knew, I was in Wilkerson's green room.

He was a gracious man, gentle but full of authority, and had a curious heart. I spent the next hour sitting with a man whose sermons had lit fires all over the world. He didn't waste time with loads of small talk either. He prophesied over me, shared his heart, laid hands on me, and imparted something into me that I still carry to this day.

What blew me away even more was that after that meeting, I'd go home and preach a message God had dropped in my spirit. A few days later, David's newsletter would show up in the mail, and it would be the same exact word, same Scripture, same burden. This parallel preaching went on for years.

There was a very real, tangible, demonstrable impartation of anointing that day.

Years later, David Patterson (who was Wilkerson's crusade director) came to work for CareCenter. So when David Wilkerson passed away, I got a call within 15 minutes of his death. I remember praying, "Lord, whatever portion is supposed to fall on us—don't let us miss it. Distribute it through us. Let that mantle land where it's supposed to." Beyond myself, I've seen that mantle upon several of the leaders that have risen up under our ministry since. I've watched it with my own eyes. Men come in broken, wild-eyed, hard—and before long, they're preaching, serving, and standing in the gap for others.

In those early days, we were just beginning to scratch the surface of what CareCenter could become. We were still connected to Church on the Rock, and Larry Lea had a heart for the poor. To put it plainly, Rockwall was an emerging and developing new money suburb, and people of that class were the main congregants at Church on the Rock. Me and our folks? Not exactly the country club types. But Larry had fire in his belly for revival, and around 1989 or so, he started pulling me into the spotlight a bit—even naming me the director of street evangelism. He would routinely highlight what we were doing in the inner city from the pulpit, as well.

One day he came to me and said, "Eldred, I want you to bring people from the inner city out here on Sunday mornings. I've already called DART (Dallas Transit system) and told them we'll cover whatever buses you need."

So I hit the streets and got to work. Three solid weeks, walking, talking, witnessing, handing out fliers and information. I didn't just fill one bus—I filled eight of those big double-sided accordion style buses, 450 people in total. Gang members, prostitutes, addicts, and ex-cons. The whole crew rolled into Rockwall like a wave.

And let me tell you, it was a sight to behold.

The next week we had a designated entrance, a roped-off hallway, and a special seating section in the sanctuary. Walkie-talkies chattered as security volunteers were on edge. There was a whole lot of fear in the room. But you know what? That first Sunday, nearly 200 people hit the altar. We didn't bring them for show, we brought them for transformation. I baptized 150 that day, and the baptistry had to be professionally cleaned, sanitized and fumigated.

We started running the "Finding the Rock" discipleship course, and I still hold the record—started with 120, finished with 119. Of course, I had a captive audience but that audience underwent a serious life change.

The truth is, our folks didn't assimilate well in that environment. They were shaving in the church bathrooms, clipping toenails in the pews. It was beautiful, messy, holy chaos. Eventually, when Larry stepped away from Church on the Rock to become a Dean at Oral Roberts University, the tide shifted. Some of the money people wanted the outreach gone, and eventually, we were released to begin what would become Hilltop Church—a local expression of the body among our culture and in our region.

I was in no way bitter. By then we were already doing a Thursday night outreach service in an old fire station in the inner city, so it made sense to launch the church full time for normal weekend services. The ministry was already independent at that point. Church on the Rock gave us a little seed money monthly—enough for a couple tanks of gas, but we were grateful for that.

We had 250 people showing up regularly on Thursday nights. One night, the presence of God fell so thick, folks outside said they saw a glory cloud hanging over the building. On another occasion, people popped inside to tell us they saw a fire inside through the windows. Miracles were popping off left and right; folks were getting saved, healed, and delivered. Eventually, we moved venues to an old pornography theater that had recently closed, where a demon-possessed dog would convulse and manifest every time we had worship. After that fell through, we shifted locations to the corner of Grand and Beacon. From there, we moved to our location on Eastside Avenue.

Of course, in those early days, I could not fully envision where things were heading or how the plan would play out. I just knew the passage in Daniel that says, "The people who know their God shall be strong, and carry out great exploits" (Daniel 11:32). That became a sort of life-verse for us.

We were running at barking dogs and taking leaps of faith that looked a little crazy. I tell my guys even now to run at the barking dog. Why? Because if the thing in front of you doesn't scare you a little, you're probably not walking by faith.

As I grew up in God, each time I'd started to get comfortable, God would call me to jump off another cliff. If He wasn't asking me to risk something, I'd get nervous, because that may just mean I had stopped listening at some point along the way.

It was hard work. Someone once asked me how many hours I worked as we pioneered the ministry. My answer: *All of them.*

Truth is, there were moments when I was fried, staring at a ceiling fan, thinking I was done. But it's in those moments— when you're out of strength, out of ideas, out of everything— that God shows up most sweetly. That's where power lives.

We must have a vision that is bigger than our bank account. We must have goals from God that overshadow our own resources. I don't know if I have ever had a plan that didn't make our board of directors break out into a sweat.

But we pray.

And we obey.

And that's the real church growth strategy.

Larry Lea once told me a story about meeting Pastor Yonggi Cho in Korea, whose church had 750,000 members at the time. He asked, "How did you build this? What's your secret?"

Cho just laughed and said, "I pray. And I obey."

Simple. Pure. Effective.

As the 1990s approached, we carried that same heartbeat into everything we did—pray, then obey. We didn't have the polish or the programs or all the features and resources we do today. We had a few simple ideas and a God who kept showing up.

CHAPTER FOUR

Here We Grow

God doesn't do ministry without doing relationships. You can have vision, passion, and even a great anointing. But if you try to walk this thing out by yourself, you're going to wear out quickly—or worse, you'll become a lone wolf that puts sheep in danger. I've seen folks with fire in their belly and no one at their side. As much as we love the idea of being warriors for Christ, this isn't a one-man battle.

When God called Nehemiah, He didn't just give him supplies. He gave him *men*—builders and fighters. Men with hammers in one hand and swords in the other, who knew how to lay bricks and swing steel. Without *people* at play, the wall never gets built and the city never gets defended. And that's exactly how God began to move in those early days of ministry for me.

I'd already had some powerful encounters—like the divine moment with David Wilkerson. But beyond the miraculous moments and strong prophecies, God was quietly sewing together relationships that would carry the weight of the ministry alongside me. Most of them didn't look like much at the time: a handshake in a prayer meeting or a brief conversation in the parking lot after. But those little moments turned into alliances that have lasted to this day. Early on I found men of prayer, men of grit—people who didn't run when it got hard. They became the scaffolding that God built CareCenter on.

And as we grew, I started to realize that God doesn't just send you people to help you build an organization, He sends people to help shape *you* in the process. I remained close with Leonard in those early days and eventually shifted from being a resident in need of help to becoming a leader under his covering. The vision called for more than just handing out food and holding church meetings. We had to open the door to real, daily transformation through discipleship. We needed a place where men could live, be discipled, be challenged, and most of all, *experience* the God of the Bible.

That's when the opportunity came.

There was an old car battery company near us owned and operated by the Covington family. It had a house on the edge of their property. It was run down, beat up, and probably unfit by city standards—but they let us use it. That was our first men's home. We didn't formally advertise nor did we stick a sign out front, but we hit the streets and, in the first week, 12 men showed up—desperate, hungry, ready or not. Eventually, that number grew as our capacity did.

We had one 30-gallon hot water heater in the home.

Let me tell you something—you haven't seen a community tested until you've got a dozen grown men fighting over a five-minute shower. They would fight and negotiate over who got to go first because those last few showers would be ice cold.

I told them, "When you start fighting over who gets to go last, I'll know you've been growing in the Lord!"

During that time, Leonard had sold everything he had and moved in with a couple from the church. It was a real act of faith; he was all-in. That left me in charge of the men's home and released more responsibility to me. The ministry life will test every part of you, especially when you're holding the keys.

Trust will nearly always be tested by temptation. New levels of responsibility will be challenged and we've got to be prepared when that happens. Back when I first got saved, before we even opened the men's home, somebody gave us an old cargo van. It was beat up and it smelled like oil and plywood, but it ran—and we were using it to haul groceries for the little food pantry we'd started. That van was a lifeline for ministry, and one day, Leonard handed me the keys.

Along with that, he also gave me an envelope with $1,200 in it. I was to drop the money off and make a food run. Leonard looked at me and said, "Go take care of it."

I remember feeling something I hadn't felt in a long time—*trusted*. I was giddy and walking light. Someone had actually handed me a vehicle, a chunk of change, and expected me to come back. Before Christ, if I'd been given that kind of freedom, I'd have disappeared—it would've been the last anyone saw of me, the van, or the cash.

So there I was—driving down the road, basking in that sense of honor, feeling like a new man.

I pulled up to a red light when out of nowhere, a blonde in a red Trans Am pulled up beside me. She looked over, made eye contact, and flashed a smile that wasn't exactly innocent.

The red light would not budge and all I could think was, *Lord, this ain't happening by accident.*

At the time, Larry Lea had been preaching a series on the weapons of our warfare. One of those messages was on temptation, sexual sin specifically. And he'd yell that phrase like a battle cry—"FLEE!"—when reading Paul's words to

Timothy: "Flee also youthful lusts; but pursue righteousness, faith, love, peace with those who call on the Lord out of a pure heart" (2 Timothy 2:22). I've come to understand that sexual temptation isn't just about sin, it's about sabotage. The enemy's not just after your purity, he's after your authority. He wants to bury you in shame so deep, you feel unworthy to speak, to lead, to even stand in a room and represent Jesus. Sometimes the fallout is even worse than the fall itself, and if you don't call it what it is, you'll start hiding. And once you start hiding, you're halfway back to who you used to be.

When I looked at that girl, I heard the swirl of biblical truths I had been learning, and more specifically, I heard Pastor Larry's voice like a cannon in my spirit—"FLEE!"

Light turned green, I punched the gas.

A few blocks down, I hit another red light, and wouldn't you know it? There she was again. I looked up and saw a hotel sitting on the corner of the intersection. She then adjusted her skirt in a way that was revealing, to say the least. There I sat, newly saved with a pile of cash, keys to a vehicle, a hotel, and a proposition.

Pastor Larry's voice boomed again, "Flee!"

Right then and there, I stomped the gas and blew through the red light without hesitation.

Call it reckless, if you will. I call it sanctified law-breaking.

That was my moment, not just to stay clean, but to choose to live *into* the reality of the man of God I was becoming. I've learned that if God can trust you in those quiet crossroads, He can trust you with people's lives.

Of course, not every test of leadership comes in that form. Some happen with blood and bruises along the way. After we had started the men's home, I learned quickly that some people require extra doses of grace. One such person— we'll call him Kent—had come into the home with a genuine hunger for God, but he was a rage-aholic, plain and simple. His existence was a product of gang rape, broken homes, unspeakable trauma. You could see the torment in his eyes— he wanted freedom but didn't know how to manage himself when the rage came on.

One day, he punched me right in the jaw.

I didn't flinch. Just looked at him and said, "My ex-old lady hits harder than that. Now get back to work."

He wasn't done. Not long after, another dispute popped up in the house. Kent got me in a headlock, and I went limp— refusing to fight back. Not because I couldn't, but because I was trying really, *really* hard to be a different man.

Afterward, I told Leonard, "He's gotta go. He's physically assaulted me multiple times. He can't stay."

Unfortunately, Leonard wouldn't put him out.

So, I took matters into my own hands and set a clear boundary. I looked the man in the eyes and said, "You put your hands on me again, you're going to the hospital. I don't have any more cheeks to turn."

Not long after, he open-hand slapped me across the face.

I walked away, went home, and told someone I trusted, "Start calling folks to get some bail money together—I'm about to go to jail."

I got in the van and drove straight to Leonard's house. I pulled up and there he was—standing in the front yard, bold as ever next to Leonard. I looked down and noticed the toolbox in the van. Flipped the lid and grabbed a crescent wrench, sliding it under my jacket.

I walked up and asked Leonard one more time, "You gonna put him out?"

"No," he said.

So I pulled that wrench out and cracked Kent across the top of the head.

Blood flew all over him and Leonard. He dropped forward, and I hit him again on the back of the head.

Leonard was six-foot-seven, 330 pounds, and he jumped on me like a linebacker. Restrained me, kept me from doing worse.

I didn't care. I had drawn a line, made a vow in my heart,

and the enemy made sure he took me to that line. They took Kent to go get stitched up, and afterward I was stripped of all ministerial authority. I was sat down and put in a disciplinary program for six months, doing reports, attending classes and counseling, staying quiet. I watched the men's home fall into chaos under new unqualified leaders who stepped in to take my place for that season.

It hurt.

But it was a good hurt.

It was a season of dealing with my anger at a core level, which *really* needed to happen. If I didn't deal with it then, it would flair up at some point and perhaps cost me even more than it did at the time.

I learned to stop justifying my anger. Prior to being sat down, my mentality was, "Well, I warned you. You should have known what I'd do!" It was my way of shifting the responsibility of my actions to the offender. But the truth is, the antagonism of the offender doesn't justify the violence of the offended.

I did not lack the encouragement of spiritual fathers during that season. We were in close relationship with a man from another ministry, and when he saw me for the first time after everything happened, he saw my countenance as I was still wrestling with my will and submission to the process. He walked up, put his arm around me, and gently said, "Come on, man."

And it hit me harder than any prophecy could have.

Sometimes, all you need is a gentle word from someone who sees your pain but won't let you sit in it.

When my six-month suspension was up, I was back to taking on more responsibility in the home. Turns out, God always circles back to test your growth. Just a few weeks after I returned, another man slapped me. I felt it in my chest—the same old fire rising. But this time, I looked at him with tears in my eyes and said, "I don't know why you're so mad, but I'm sorry. I love you. And there's nothing you can do to change that."

In the decades I've been in ministry since, I have not been physically assaulted a single time since that incident. It was truly an era of testing.

And the man I hit with a wrench? I still love him and we patched things up. Over time, he healed—inside and out. In fact, he went back to school, got his drug and alcohol recovery license, and worked for the Salvation Army as a counselor for years. When he had to write a paper on his hero to finish his coursework, he wrote about me.

In the paper he said, "Eldred was the only man who ever told me exactly what he'd do—and then did it."

It wasn't the best way to be featured in a "hero" story, but it was real. It's just how God works: He builds trust, even through our faults and failures.

* * *

For a good while after I got saved, folks from my old life figured me and the kids had just disappeared. And in a way, we had. Paul said, "Reckon yourselves to be dead indeed to sin, but alive to God in Jesus Christ our Lord" (Romans 6:11). I didn't just leave my old lifestyle, I died to it. And when you're dead to something, it eventually quits looking for you.

Old family, old friends—they faded into the rearview. Austin, my older half brother, figured my faith was just a phase. He didn't buy into words, only watched for fruit. For him it took seven years before he called me out of the blue. "I'm calling because I believe what you're doing is real," he said. "I'm proud of you. I want you and your family to come to Thanksgiving at our house."

Now, you don't know him, but let me tell you—that phone call was a miracle in itself. Nothing I could have said would've convinced him. But my life, quiet and consistent, had done what no promises or pleas could. God doesn't just rebuild you, but He restores your reputation.

Part of leaving behind old relationships and influences

means gaining new ones. When I was first getting my life in order, I hadn't given any thought to marriage. I'd been through enough dysfunctional relationships to know that just being "in love" won't cut it. I was focused on my kids, on ministry, and on staying clean. Val was out of the picture by then, and I wasn't out looking for a wife, to say the least. I tell my guys all the time that Adam was sleeping when God gave him his wife.

Then I ended up in an Overcomers meeting in Mesquite, and Richard Stakes was preaching one of his fire-breathing messages. I noticed a woman in the room—Jean Marie— weeping under the weight of the Word. The second I saw her, I heard a word in my spirit: "Wife."

I wanted no part of that marriage business. I'd been there, done that, and had the scars to prove it.

After the meeting, I patted her gently on the shoulder, rationalizing she was someone else's wife, and said, "God sees your heart. It's gonna be okay." Then I turned and kept my distance.

About a month later, I got a call from the lady working the front desk at our food pantry. "I've got a young woman here with her little girl," she said. "They have a Christmas tree they want to give away. I thought about your kids and the men in the home."

"Sure," I said, "send 'em over."

Fifteen minutes later, that same girl, Jean Marie, was standing at my front door. And let me tell you, I was not ready. She looked *good*. I was stumbling around, trying to help set up the tree, dropping ornaments and stuttering like a school boy. Needless to say, we started courting after that meeting.

We got to know each other fast. She had come out of addiction herself and had her own story, her own wounds. It was clear from the start that she had a heart for the Lord and wasn't playing games. She was a single mom, living with her folks, and riding the bus to work. The reason? She had given her car away to help someone else. Most single moms would be eager to receive free gifts; meanwhile, Jean Marie gave them. It's just who she was.

Our proposal wasn't fancy. After seven or eight months of courting, we were driving down the road, on the way to a speaking engagement. I looked at her and said, "Hey girl, you gonna marry me or not? Because if not, I'm done."

Not exactly candlelight and roses, but it worked.

We married on July 3, 1988, after the first men's home was up and running for only about a year. We had our wedding at 2 o'clock on Sunday afternoon during our weekly Overcomers meeting. Charles and Sharon Burton, who were like a mom and dad to most of us, led the ceremony. They were staff pastors at Church on the Rock, and the leaders of the Overcomers ministry. There were probably 250 people there—several of them part of our growing crew at CareCenter.

Some folks in the church pooled money together and sent us on a trip to Cancun for our honeymoon. Jean chipped in, too—she was working at the time, and the plan was for her to keep working to help support things, as I had no income from the ministry. Her job lasted about four months before it became clear that God had other plans. We weren't just building a marriage, we were building a ministry, and it was going to take both of us full-time.

We lived by faith, raised our kids in the men's home, shared our table with broken men, and trusted God to provide. Jean Marie and I brought our families together—Lonnie, Meredith, and Jeri Quin, Jean's daughter. Later, we began having children of our own. Rebecca Danielle, our first, came along two years into the marriage. Two years later, her brother Caleb was born. And ten years into our marriage— right when we thought we were done—we had Naomi, and finally, Dannah, our last, when we were both forty-four. We lovingly refer to them as our second litter.

We didn't do things in the traditional order from the get go. We didn't have a 401K or matching furniture, but we had God, a high calling, and each other.

Most days' provision was a literal miracle and often required some resourceful creativity. I remember someone from Jack in the Box got wind of what we were doing and offered us boxes upon boxes of taco meat. So much so that we had to source off-site freezers to store the stuff. At that time, we'd take food donations from absolutely anywhere. If it was edible, we'd eat it. If it was close, we'd pray over it and make it work.

Initially I was thrilled thinking this ground beef would feed us comfortably for months. Turns out, the meat was a bad batch. It had been over-seasoned so badly it was almost inedible, so they figured it was better to give it to us than to throw it out. After some experimentation, we figured out if you put it in a colander and ran it under water, you could rinse off just enough salt and spice to make it work. We'd grab some tortillas and make do. That was breakfast, lunch, and dinner for a long time.

Needless to say, when we came out of those lean seasons, Jack in the Box was not first on my list of restaurants to dine in.

Through the scarce and difficult times, Jean Marie showed us all a masterclass in grateful servanthood. She would tell you she embraced her missionary calling before we ever met—and after we met, the calling crystalized as missionary work to the inner city.

There is not another woman on this earth who could have stepped into the position Jean Marie did in those early years. We had nothing. We lived in the men's home and trusted God for every single thing. She stood strong, never asked for the spotlight, never needed a microphone, and never once complained. She is maternal, fierce, and unshakable. She raised our kids, kept the house, served the ministry, and did so with joy.

She saw what many did not: the big picture. She knew we weren't just scraping by for the sake of being sacrificial but that we were building something that would outlive us. And she knew that building would take time, sacrifice, and a deep measure of faith. It wound up being nine years before we were able to receive any financial compensation from the ministry. We were building and raising a family, depending on miraculous provision everyday. I could never have walked this walk without that girl. She embodies the grace of Jesus, and while she's never tried to take credit, I can plainly say that what's been built has been built by us *together*, and yet in spite of us. Her quiet strength has carried more of the ministry than most will ever know.

One of the earliest moments I saw that strength in action was during our very first Thanksgiving outreach in the late 1980s. Jean Marie and I were newly married. We already had the men's home going, and I felt the weight of wanting something for people who had never experienced family on that holiday. Not just food—but belonging, dignity, trust. Our original plan was modest: feed residents, their families, and the children of our staff. A headcount of thirty in total. Jean Marie, her sister Jacquelyn, and a missionary named Mary Alice agreed to step up and help cook and facilitate the dinner. The ladies organized the operation and in kitchens across Dallas, turkeys would be cooking overnight in the ovens of about everyone we knew. The plan was simple, heartfelt, but limited.

Then God began stretching us.

One evening, I came home and said, "God put it on my heart: we should reach out to men in nearby bars—men who would otherwise sit alone without a meal on Thanksgiving." We mused: can we add food for another thirty? Then I came back again with a bigger ask: "We need to take it beyond bars to the highways and byways—we should invite everyone who needs a meal." The stretch wasn't small. We'd have to trust God for over a hundred meals. We were exhausted and resource-poor, but we obeyed.

I made some Xeroxed flyers (ugly black-and-white things) and started passing them out to the homeless, telling them we'd be doing a Thanksgiving meal on Saturday after the holiday. We'd have vans to pick them up, bring them to a location, and feed them like family. I didn't know where the food would come from, or the vans for that matter. I just knew I had to obey.

The funds were just not there to purchase a bunch of meals for the event, and no other resources were in sight. The week before the holiday, I still did not have a solution.

Thursday, which was Thanksgiving day—we still had no food.

Friday came. Nothing.

The event had been highly publicized by our team and we had less than 24 hours to come up with a meal plan.

That Saturday, before the official outreach, Jim—Jean Marie's sister's husband and a bartender for the Stoneleigh Hotel—pulled up in a limousine at the hotel. He came to fetch food supplies for our outreach. As he waited, the chef packed the car full, then dispatched a catering truck behind Jim's limo with even more food.

It was all there: Turkey, dressing, all the trimmings, desserts, plus all the birds that Jean Marie and the ladies had cooking around town.

That Saturday morning, we picked up 120 people with borrowed vans and fed them a five-star meal—for free. Beyond physical food, we served spiritual nourishment as well.

We prayed, preached, hugged, and shared. God had shown up, right on time, and provided in a way that we could not have planned nor predicted. And that outreach became a tradition, one that has grown year after year.

We have hundreds of volunteers and interns who participate annually, some for one-off events, others on an ongoing basis. We have people participating from various denominations and circles within the body of Christ. What started as a single dinner at one location has evolved into packing and hand-delivering 1,500 boxes of Thanksgiving groceries door to door, by a team of volunteers who pray and share at the doorsteps of the recipients. And still the provision for this is always by faith and supernatural supply.

Looking back, I see that the small band of women saying "yes," the fliers, the limousine pulling up at Stoneleigh—it was all part of a Kingdom equation. We learned early that the call doesn't always make sense. But obeying in our smallness opens room for God's greatness.

We've come to realize if it doesn't demand a stretching kind of faith, it doesn't produce a supernatural result. With CareCenter, whatever we had, we gave. Often when it didn't even make sense. Whether it's our Soul Snatchers outreach, where we set up a BBQ pit and give away food and offer the gospel, or our after school programs, our goal was always the same: build trust, meet needs, and offer the gospel. Jesus didn't say, "Throw baitless hooks." He said, "I'll make you fishers of men." And every fisherman knows, you don't catch anything if you don't know what bait to use.

The services we offer, our food pantry, men's and women's homes, programs, they're not the main thing. They're the invitation—the bait. The main thing is always Jesus, His Great Commission, and inviting the masses to sit at the table.

It doesn't wrestle folks into submission. It sets a table, lays out the meal, and says, "Come and eat."

I learned that lesson a long time ago.

When I was about 4 years old, I had a little pet parakeet. Unsatisfied with his water intake, I decided to try to help him have a drink, but he wasn't taking any in. So I grabbed his tiny head, dipped it down into the water bowl—trying to force it—and held it there just a bit too long. As you might guess, he stopped moving shortly after and drowned in my hand. I wasn't trying to hurt him. In fact, I thought I was helping. But what I thought was care was actually force, and my good intentions killed the bird.

That lesson stuck with me. I never forgot the feeling of holding something fragile and thinking I was helping, only to realize I was hurting. Ministry can work the same way if you're not careful. You can love people so much that you try to force them into healing, force them into freedom, or force them into faith. But that's not how the gospel works.

The gospel is always invitation, not imposition.

We don't force people to be discipled as this only results in hurt. We don't drag folks into the kingdom. I've watched leaders—myself included—cross that same line, trying to make people grow faster than they're ready. But thankfully, the Lord taught us another way. We've made our paradigm about preparing a place for people rather than pushing people into a mold. This means we move from grabbing and pulling to offering and inviting.

Because if the gospel isn't received freely, it's usually not received at all.

CHAPTER FIVE

New Territory

We all remember David's anointing by Samuel as he stood among his brothers. This initial splash of oil designated him as a future king and graced him with what he needed to kill a giant, honor Saul, and take care of the preparatory work prior to sitting on a throne. However, there are lesser known anointings that took place in David's life, *three* in total.

The second anointing came when he was made king over Judah. In other words, the anointing allowed him to step into a *partial* leadership over the kingdom he was promised. Eventually, the third anointing came as he entered rulership over *all* of Israel—the full promise. Each anointing wasn't just a pat on the back or a "go get 'em!" It was preparation for the pressure that came with the next season. *The first anointing marked him. The second one tested him. The third one established him.*

I believe God works the same way in us. He anoints us in stages, not just to elevate us but to stretch us. Every new level of responsibility comes with new weight. And if He doesn't anoint you for the task, it'll crush you.

As I moved beyond spiritual infancy in the 1980s and into more maturity, new measures of leadership fell into my lap. By 1993, Leonard was preparing to step away from the ministry altogether for personal reasons. The initial seven years of toil, lack, and sacrifice had taken its toll on him and his family. They had poured themselves out and he was set to hand me the reins. In terms of selection, there wasn't a vote or a power grab—I was simply the one standing. During the previous years, with its trials, temptations, and *yes* even failures, I had been anointed for expanded responsibility.

We formed a presbytery of city leaders to help guide us during the transition. One of the greatest gifts God ever gave me—beyond buildings, beyond provision—was spiritual fathers. Men like Robert Summers, Joe Martin, Gene Lewis, and Terry Moore. Each one brought something different into my life. Wisdom, affirmation, correction at times. I'll never forget one of those fathers—Robert Summers—who had a tall, steady presence like a mountain. I was in my thirties, and every time he'd hug me, he'd rest my head against his chest, and in that place I could hear his heart beat and feel the weight of his covering. He'd say, "Proud of you, Eldred." And it wasn't just gooey sentiment—it was the outflowing of the Father's love. That kind of blessing shapes a man and settles his soul.

I had also met Pastor Terry Moore at a monthly prayer meeting in the 1980s and we connected right away. He and Sojourn Church became faithful supporters of CareCenter, which remains the case even to this day. He is my pastor and spiritual covering. They cared about the ministry, yes, but they also cared about our family at the helm of the ministry. On one occasion in the early days, I recall not knowing what I could do for my children for Christmas. On December 23, a van of volunteers pulled up from Sojourn Church and gave us a check.

Pastor Terry's support has been steady through the years, but it was particularly critical during my transition into heading up CareCenter. Reason being, there will always be some vulnerability before, during, and after a big regime change. The presbytery around me often gave counsel that I was too green to know I needed at the time, but I embraced it.

I wasn't handed a golden baton; I was handed a ministry

with a lot of potential, but a lot of mess to go with it. There were debts, broken-down buildings, and a crew of recovering men that barely knew how to spell "disciple." But there was something else too: an unfailing promise from God.

There was no guaranteed salary or perk package. In fact, as previously mentioned, for the first nine years, we didn't take a salary from the ministry at all, and frankly, I'm convinced that we weren't ready for it. Coming from my background, I might not have been able to handle a pocket full of money.

So we pressed on by faith, making sacrifices and allowing ourselves to suffer for the call. It reminded me of what the Lord said to Paul: "I'll show you what you must suffer" (see Acts 9:16). That was essentially Paul's ordination service, and I can relate to the sentiment.

After looking at the financial state of the ministry, I knew we might not be able to dig our way out, but we could *give* our way out. You cannot lead without giving. It doesn't matter how much vision you have, if you're not willing to give first, you'll never have the authority to lead others. And it's not just about tithes, it's about living open-handed with everything: your time, your energy, or your last ten dollar bill.

Looking at our negative balance sheet, a spiritual father, Gene Lewis, pulled me aside and said, "Start giving 10 percent off the ministry income itself. And give Leonard six months of financial support as he transitions."

I looked at him like he was crazy.

I said, "We don't even have money to pay ourselves, and you want me to give away a tenth, and pay Leonard too?"

He said, "Just do it."

So we did. We tithed the first fruit off every bean we counted, made a commitment to Leonard as a pure act of obedience, not knowing how we would pull it off.

Every Monday we'd sit down, go through the available funds, and pull the first 10 percent off the top before *anything* was sent elsewhere—bills included. It's called the first fruits for a reason. Then we'd start working through the bills, the debts, and the occasional angry vendors. I'd drive around town making apologies and handing out cash where I could, trying to rebuild relationships with folks we owed. After that, I'd take a hundred dollar bill, put it aside for the gas tank, and say, "Alright Lord, let's go again for another week!" And somehow, we met our commitment to Leonard every month.

We stuck with this illogical generosity for two years. In 1995, I had a dream that changed everything. In the dream, I was in a room full of church people—folks I recognized. The door busted open and this massive man stormed in, looking like an old WWF wrestler. He started tearing the place up, trying to get to the people. I fought him off, getting exhausted, worn down. Finally, I looked down and saw a hammer on the table. I grabbed it and hit him in the head, and he dropped. I supposed the Lord decided to speak in a way I could understand.

When I woke up, the Lord spoke: "The spirit of poverty is broken off this ministry."

That Sunday I preached on *breaking a spirit of poverty* and something wild happened—the offering doubled. But it wasn't a one-time bump. From that day forward, our giving never went back down again.

Obedience had opened something in the spirit.

We desperately needed this breakthrough against the poverty spirit. As one of my elders said, "You are the poor trying to help the poor." From the start my heart has been for the poor and the fatherless. Poverty is not a number in a bank account, it's a mindset. There is inferiority and shame that go along with poverty thinking that weasels its way into other areas of life. My passion and burden was to help people move from a lens of lack to an attitude of abundance, and *abundance* did not necessarily mean a fat paycheck but an understanding that the children of God can expect the provision of God.

Provision has always been part of the story. From the very

beginning, there's been a flow, a kind of exchange between heaven and earth. We obey, God responds. We give, He multiplies. The *faith up, favor down* flow has marked this ministry more times than I can count. Now and then, that provision doesn't come with fire from heaven—it comes with a knock on the door or the rumble of a truck.

There were mornings where we would gather, and we'd already made the decision to fast—not for spiritual breakthrough, but because there was no food in the pantry. When we prayed, "Give us this day our daily bread," it wasn't an allegory. We needed actual bread. During one of those early morning prayer sessions, as we prayed for something to eat, a man in a van pulled up. He got out and said, "Yesterday, the Lord told me to fill this van with food and bring it to you." We didn't know him. We had no prior connection. But that van was full of groceries—and that's what kept us going. That kind of spontaneous provision happened all the time. You don't learn trust like that from a book. You learn it on your knees. When God shows up like that, time and time again, you don't just believe in miracles, you start expecting them.

On another occasion, a man pulled up in front of the men's home with a truck and trailer full of lawn equipment. He stepped out, said he'd heard what we were doing, and told me something I'll never forget: "We're missionaries, heading to Chad. We're leaving everything behind and won't be coming back." He went on to explain that he built a full service lawn business with 40 residential contracts.

"I'd like to give you the business," he said, "and I'll stick around for a month and train you and your guys in how to be a lawn crew."

That day he handed me his entire business—mowers, blowers, edgers, weed wackers, gas cans, a trailer, his truck, contracts, and all.

After a month, he left for Africa, and we had ourselves a functional lawn crew with 40 contracts, each bringing in $25 per week, which was a massive windfall at the time. It became more than money, though. That lawn service became a discipleship tool. It taught these men how to show up, how to sweat, how to submit to authority. It taught them that work was holy and that dignity doesn't come from a title, it comes from effort.

We didn't let anyone get soft. I'd tell the guys, "If you stand around on the job with your hands in your pockets, don't come belly up to the table at dinner."

Paul said, "If a man will not work, he doesn't eat" (see 2 Thessalonians 3:10).

Of course, when you take a group of men out of the home and introduce them to a hard day's work, it creates room for some fussing. Now and then a guy would complain, "We work for free!"

"Hold up," I'd say. "Let's break down what you cost versus what you bring in."

From there we calculated transportation, food, housing, classes—and every time, they were in the hole. It wasn't slavery, it was structure. Apostolic fathering means making men out of boys, both in the spirit and in their natural work. John Kelly used to say, "I shouldn't have to flirt with a man to get him to move chairs." The beauty of the lawn business is it taught the value of labor, servanthood, and institutional authority. It taught men how to start again. We didn't just cut lawns, we cut ties with poverty mindsets.

With our ministry, we made it a goal to turn every donated dollar into five. How? Generosity, stewardship, efficiency, labor, and stretching every dollar we got. When Jesus fed the 5,000 men and their families in Matthew 14:15–16, the disciples were trying to figure out how they would feed such a big crowd with such limited resources. Jesus gave a simple five-word reply that has guided my life: "Bring them here to me" (speaking of the five loaves and two fish). From there, He multiplied what they had as they got their eyes off of what they didn't.

That same principle became the foundation of how we

operated—from the food pantry to the lawn business. We didn't wait for ideal conditions; we worked with what we had and let God breathe on it. Eventually, we expanded the cottage industry into irrigation, added two more crews, and took on more and more contracts. It was one of the best discipleship programs we ever ran, and it's still going today—40 years later.

Between the church, food pantry, outreaches, and lawn services, CareCenter was firing on all cylinders. We would pick up bulk food at 14 cents a pound from the North Texas Food Bank for distribution and made a connection early on with a catering company. After corporate events or weddings, they would have boxes of leftover foods—tamales, casseroles, breakfast sandwiches, pasta trays, roasted chicken, rolls, and the occasional boxes of gourmet desserts.

In those days, we operated out of our main campus on Eastside Avenue, a location that had become both a base of ministry and a battle zone. That property had been donated to us in 1990, during the fallout of the savings and loan crisis. The Resolution Trust Corporation, a government agency set up to liquidate failed properties, had opened a door for nonprofits to take over distressed sites. Ours was one of them. It was a horseshoe-shaped property consisting of 10 duplexes, gutted, stripped bare, and filled with homeless people when we first stepped in. But we saw potential.

We turned it into a hub: food distribution, residential housing, offices. We tied two buildings together that became our church. We built a place where ministry could flow seven days a week.

But not everyone wanted us there.

An urban renewal board in Dallas—unelected developers with power granted by the city—started targeting properties like ours. They'd meet in city council chambers with the authority to condemn sites. I watched them condemn a widow's property that she had lived in and raised her family in for 50 years. They would raze them, charge the owner with demolition fees, and develop them into condos and so forth. It was blatant corruption. They fought us hard, giving us unrealistic deadlines to meet certain codes, threats, penalties, and ultimately tried to back us into a corner. We had a pro bono attorney doing his best, but nothing clicked and the pressure remained.

Then Robert Summers made a call. He had a personal relationship with the mayor of Dallas, and after one conversation, the pressure stopped. The city backed off. We kept the property, we renovated it, and we operated out of that place for 15 years.

Later on, we acquired three more acres next door, and the value just kept going up. What started as a broken-down shell became a sanctuary—a place of healing, training, and transformation. It was a fight to keep it, but it became proof that God plants His people where the enemy tries to uproot them.

* * *

Suffering. It's a word most folks would rather avoid—until they can't. You can ignore it, deny it, or try to rebuke it. But at some point, suffering walks right in and sits at your table. The truth is, suffering is essential. It's part of our warfare as believers, and how we embrace it matters deeply.

I recently obtained an authentic Mexican molcajete, and part of the seasoning process that readies the bowl for use is to crush rice and salt into the pores. Because it's made of lava stone, if you don't take the crushing step first, the bowl can come apart and you end up with rocky grit in your food. Crushing is simply part of the process of preparing the instrument for use. Most certainly, crushing is part of the process in our lives as believers as we are readied for use, as well.

I learned this principle in the fire of ministry early on. We were packed with 30 to 40 men in the home, working to keep them fed and discipled. Meanwhile the crack epidemic was ripping through our neighborhood, and the demand for what we offered was sometimes more than we could supply.

We were believing God for everything from toilet paper to basic meals. Some folks in the church were concerned and informed me I should get a "job." One brother said I was worse than an infidel because I wasn't providing like he thought I should. But I was working 100 hours a week, in the field God had given me, seeing abundant fruit and clinging to the promises of God. Our needs were met miraculously.

Over the years I have reminded myself of a message Larry Lea preached on warfare. He was teaching on the familiar weapons of the Word, the blood, and so forth. When I went home that night, I was reading from 1 Peter 4:1 (PARA): "Just as Christ suffered in the flesh, arm yourself with the same purpose." That phrase hit me so hard, I pulled out my Strong's Concordance, and what I found changed my theology for good. That word *arm* means to "equip yourself with the weapon of"—and in context, it is the weapon of suffering. I'd never heard that before, but it was right there in front of me. In that moment, the Lord gave me a vision of a sword. He said, "Eldred, if you hold the sword by the grip, it will become an offensive weapon against your adversaries. But if you turn it and hold the suffering improperly with the blade, it'll cut you to shreds."

In other words, how you handle your suffering determines whether it becomes a weapon or a wound.

We don't rejoice in suffering because we're masochists. We rejoice because it's *producing* something. Paul said in Colossians 1:24 (PARA), "I rejoice in my sufferings for your sake, and in my flesh I fill up what is lacking in the afflictions of Christ, for the sake of his body, which is the church." Throughout Scripture I began to notice instruction like "count it joy," or rejoice, in the context of suffering, affliction, and trials, with an exhortation to know that it was producing something that would bring Him glory and bring maturity and growth to the believer. That's not popular theology, but it's real. We could call this the theology of *redemptive* suffering. We can live life and allow the pain to harden us or humble us, and every time we choose the second option, the power of Christ shows up and works through us.

One time I was with a man who raised horses. I was nitpicking this horse, looking it over to try to find some hidden flaw. The old man looked at me and said, "You don't have to go looking for problems. If they're there, they'll show themselves." That's exactly how I feel about suffering. I don't go looking for it. But when it comes, I want to be the kind of man who's not surprised by it. I want a doctrine and a devotion that doesn't collapse when things get hard.

"Dear friends, don't be surprised at the fiery trials you are going through, as if something strange were happening to

you. Instead, be very glad—for these trials make you part-ners with Christ in his suffering, so that you will have the wonderful joy of seeing his glory when it is revealed to all the world." (1 Peter 4:12–13 NLT)

You can't shortcut this process. If you try to escape it too early, you miss what God wanted to extract. There's no oil unless something gets crushed, which is the pattern all through Scripture. Broken bread. Crushed grapes. A pierced side. And then *resurrection*.

Don't waste your suffering. Learn to hold it properly.

"...that I may know Him and the power of His resurrec-tion, and the fellowship of His sufferings, being conformed to His death, if, by any means, I may attain to the resur-rection from the dead. (Philippians 3:10–11)

One of the challenges that comes with this call is that suf-fering doesn't just fall on your shoulders—it bleeds into the lives of those closest to you. Especially when you're pioneer-ing a ministry in one hand and trying to hold your family together in the other. If you suffer, they do too.

When I stepped into leadership, I had an anointing and revelatory blueprint on how to build the ministry He had given me. What I didn't know—what I completely failed to understand—was that God didn't just call me; He called *us*.

Jean Marie, the kids, we were a package deal. We weren't just a family, but a team, built and placed together by God to carry something sacred. But back then, I didn't see it. I thought if I handled the ministry part, they would fall in line. I didn't disciple my kids into the cost of walking with Jesus, nor did I bring them along with clarity. Instead, I expected them to suck it up and follow along. I was at the helm, full throttle, head down in the vision, and I left pieces of them behind in the process.

Any pastor who raises children knows that kids have a radar for hypocrisy. They might not say it, but they see it. They don't care how fiery you preach on Sunday if the house is cold on Monday. I often disciplined out of anger and was prone to being too harsh. They saw my anger—what they couldn't see was the fear underneath it. They didn't quite grasp that I knew what it was like to reject authority, reject God, and leap into the deep end without any idea how to swim. My stern correction of them was often a fear of them duplicating my mistakes, rather than a loving discipline toward the feet of Jesus. Grace can be easy to preach in the pulpit but difficult to display in the home.

At times our daughter Meredith resented the ministry and felt a jealousy toward it. She was 6 when I came to Christ and began pioneering. In her mother's absence, she embraced a very maternal role over her brother Lonnie. It was just us three against the world. After I began the ministry, and eventually married Jean, those dynamics obviously changed. Her jealousy turned bitter, and that bitterness showed up in rebellion. I am thankful to say that rebellion turned around; she came home after her own wilderness experience. She worked for me for five years as the best director of operations I've ever had, before having to step away for health reasons. She also gave me three beautiful grandchildren and named her son after me.

Our son Lonnie was sweet-natured from the start, but he had his own way of thinking and could be wild and defiant at times. I rarely handled that properly either, fearing he would become what I had been. I often overcorrected—not out of love, but out of embarrassment and fear. The kids became extensions of my reputation instead of reflections of their own process.

I can look back now, particularly in those early years, and say I missed it most of the time. I was intense and held high expectations. It came from my upbringing, my culture, and frankly, how I'm wired. Years later I took a Life Languages test and found out only 6 percent of the population is wired like I am. I'm a high mover, meaning I get things done, to put it plainly. I get people unstuck, if you will. Of course, that same drive that built a ministry can bulldoze the ones you love. I would pray and cry out to God, "Lord, help me to help them. Empower me to be the father I did not have." Up until then, I simply had no tools, grid, or understanding of what fatherhood should look like. I was learning on the fly.

Over time, I learned to lead differently. Forty years of preaching and pioneering will humble you. I've had to learn how to come alongside people, not just pull them up. I can now say "I'm with you" instead of "Get it together." I've learned to put a hand on a shoulder instead of just pointing the way. I still have to engage in unsticking things at times, but I definitely have more patience in the process.

But I'll be the first to admit, I didn't start that way, though I refuse to live in regret or under some harsh scrutiny of my past. Where I was weak, He was strong. The same miracles we were seeing in and through the ministry, we were seeing in and through our own home and family.

By 1996 the ministry had grown to where I could finally receive a very modest salary. Jean Marie and I were ready to move out of the men's home and into a place of our own. We found a house about a mile from the ministry property—a place to raise our kids and catch our breath. The problem? I had no credit and no W2s. I'd worked my tail off for nine years, but not one minute of it was documented in the eyes of the system. Still, God made a way with another miracle. It became a testimony of God's faithfulness and provision as we explained to the underwriters how we survived, and others wrote letters attesting to it. Miraculously, we got approved, bought the home, and once again miraculously, within four years it had doubled in value.

Those same years, we saw a powerful move of the Spirit. For three straight years, the presence of God was thick. Lives were being changed. Chains were breaking. But not everything was easy. As often happens when God moves, people come in with agendas. We went through church splits and betrayal. I had one man I brought in close, which means he was close enough to put a knife in my back. And he did. That season taught me more about forgiveness, boundaries, and trusting God with the fallout than any sermon I'd ever preached. It was a hard, refining, and absolutely glorious time.

And while all that was unfolding publicly, God was still doing private miracles in our home. When Rebecca, our first daughter was born, she was healthy at first. But in the hospital nursery, she started turning blue. They found a valve in her heart that only had a pinhole opening and discovered her heart was enlarged. Baylor rushed her to Children's Hospital for emergency surgery. They cut through her breastbone and put her in NICU. Tubes, machines—she was ten days old and fighting for her life.

They had to do a second open-heart surgery on day eight to repair more of the damage. And during that stretch, I went into the hospital chapel and spoke one of the rawest decrees of my life. I said, "Let me tell you something, devil—if this child dies, I'll gather every outlaw you can imagine and preach the gospel to them, and you know if I do, they will get saved."

I wasn't bluffing.

We leaned on Jesus; what else did we have? The men in the home rallied, fasted, and prayed like warriors on a mission. Shortly after, Rebecca pulled through and has had a normal, healthy life ever since with no issues. She is a walking miracle.

Then came our boy Caleb. They pulled us into a room after a prenatal scan and told us he had a growth on the end of his brain, the kind that leads to what they call hydrocephalus or "water head." The doctor—a Christian man who had done all our prenatal care and delivery—told us the outlook was grim. Most kids with that condition don't live beyond 12. He gently told us we should prepare ourselves—that our boy would likely be mentally disabled during the course of his short life.

I looked at him and said, "That's not gonna happen."

We called people to pray. Some fasted. We stood in the gap. As soon as Caleb was born, they rushed him out for a CT scan. That man came back, white as a sheet, and said, "This is miraculous." The scan was clear. There was absolutely nothing wrong with our son in any way, shape, or form.

To top it off, those doctors never charged us a dime for the birth of our kids, which is the kind of provision God pours out when you've got no safety net but Him. Those were the moments that cemented my conviction: obedience will bring provision, and suffering is part of the price.

When Naomi came along, she was a breath of fresh air. More like Jean than me, she was sweet, considerate, honoring, and eager to please. A typical middle child. The kids used to say, "Dad, we know Naomi is your favorite." Of course, I would defend it. "No, I love you all the same." In truth it wasn't my love that was different, but Naomi was different and easier. Later after they all were grown, they would say, "We know Naomi is your favorite," and I'd say, "Well, duh," which was a running family joke. Naomi and her husband Lalo have given us three beautiful grandchildren, as well.

Looking back, it's clear to me that God was writing a story bigger than we understood. From healing miracles to financial ones, every moment was a reminder that when you walk by faith, you don't walk alone. I was by no means a perfect parent, but I learned to trust God to fill in the gaps. He did more than that; He showed Himself faithful in ways we'll never forget. And as our kids grew, so did our understanding: obedience doesn't always make the path easy, but it does keep you on the path where miracles happen.

CHAPTER SIX

On Purpose

There is a kind of tiredness that sleep and a vacation won't fix. There comes a point in ministry where miracles aren't enough for you to ride on. It's a place where fruit on the outside does not solve your fatigue on the inside. The anointing still flows, but your soul feels dry. I hit that wall hard on a number of occasions over the years.

In the early days, I walked into Robert Summers's office one afternoon and dropped the bomb. "I'm resigning. I'm out. I'm done with all this." I was worn thin. Tired of the weight. Tired of the expectations. I didn't want to be a disappointment, but I didn't want to pretend I could carry it anymore either. What I expected was a bit of sympathy—a shoulder, a pat on the back, maybe even permission to ditch the whole operation.

What I got instead was the *truth*.

Robert looked at me and said, "Eldred, who exactly are you resigning to? Because I didn't call you into ministry, so I cannot accept your resignation. You need to go do business with God, buddy."

That cut me clean—because he was right. How could I tell a board I was leaving when that board had not called me to begin with?

Around that same time, Gary Turner, one of my early friends and a fellow pioneer, heard I was unraveling and came to find me. He could see I was about to bail and I told him flat out, "I'm leaving, man. Don't try to stop me. I'm going to work."

My plan was not to go off in some sort of carnal, sinful rebellion. I was simply tired of being blistered by the ministry without the personal provision to prove it. Gary didn't back down and asked me what I was going to do. Sarcastically, I popped off and said, "I'm gonna buy me a watch."

We wrapped up the conversation, he offered a few words of encouragement, and we went our separate ways. I wasn't convinced to stay but I appreciated that he showed up.

Later that day, I came back to where we'd been talking.

Sitting on the table was Gary's $500 watch he had slipped off and left behind without a comment. Boy, I felt like a worm. It wrecked me. Not because of the monetary value, but because of the selfless love behind it. That gesture cut through all the noise in my head. It was like God saying, "I still see you."

First the dirt bike with Austin as a teen, and now the watch with Gary—God had a way of taking my sarcastic deflection and answering it with something deeper. He wasn't just giving me a piece of jewelry, He was pointing me past my temporary wants to a greater truth: *You are seen. You are known. And you are not alone.*

Gary passed away from a heart attack suddenly at 34 years of age, just a couple of years after our conversation, leaving behind his wife and small children.

But the story does not end there.

Years later, I was at a conference. When the offering was being taken, the Lord spoke to me: "Put your watch in the offering." I certainly did not want to. I loved that watch and had quite the personal history with it. But I obeyed. What I did not know at the time was that the man leading the conference (Gary's spiritual father, Gene Lewis) had actually given that watch to Gary many, many years prior. When they counted the offering, Gene Lewis looked down and said, "I know this watch."

The original gift he had given was now back in his hands. Later when Gary's adult son was placed into ministry, Gene handed the watch to him during the ordination.

God has a way of bringing things full circle and using our lowest points to create a whole host of divine orchestrations.

What I learned during that time was simple but costly: obedience is how you hold on when your hands are tired, when the pressure doesn't let up, when the promises feel heavy, when the warfare outweighs the applause. That's when you find out if you just have a job or a true calling.

If you're called, you can try to quit, but the call won't let you. Paul said, "For the gifts and the calling of God are irrevocable" (Romans 11:29). That word—*irrevocable*—in the Greek is *ametamelētos*. It means without regret, without changing one's mind, without reversal.

In other words, when God calls you, He doesn't flinch later and take it back. He doesn't look at your past, your failures, or your worst days and say, "Yeah, I probably shouldn't have picked that one."

He knew exactly who He was getting when He called you.

That term *irrevocable* is a legal term, too. Like something written into covenant that can't be undone. You can run, rebel, mess it up—but that call stays active. You might go silent, but the call does not. That purpose is still humming in your spirit like an engine waiting to turn over. That's why I couldn't quit, because deep down, I knew God hadn't changed His mind about me, even when I had.

Some folks might look at the ups and downs of my life and label it as some kind of bipolar reaction. Many don't understand the weight that comes with apostolic calling— the birthing, the pioneering, the stretching. There are days when you stare up at the ceiling fan and think, "I can't do this anymore." You don't want to abandon the call, but you don't know how to survive it either. Then the next day, you have more zeal and passion for the things of God than when you first got saved.

I've walked through seasons of Holy Ghost fire and seasons of depression, back-to-back. I've seen that same cycle in men and women who carry authority in the gospel. There's always death in your body before there's resurrection power through it.

Paul put it like this: "Always carrying about in the body the dying of the Lord Jesus, that the life of Jesus also may be manifested in our body" (2 Corinthians 4:10). That phrase "carrying about" in the Greek is *periphero*, which means to continually bear, to wear it like a garment, something you don't set down when it gets heavy. And "the dying" is *nekrō-sis*—a *death work*, an ongoing process, not just one moment of surrender but a lifestyle of laying it down.

We carry death so that life itself shows up through us. The Friday on the cross has to precede the resurrection on Sunday. It's not a theory but a living reality in our lives and ministries. *The gospel comes alive in other people through the stuff that dies in you.*

Jean and I joke that the only reason we're still doing this is because "we never felt like quitting on the same day."

But deep down, we stayed because of one thing: purpose, and obedience to it.

Not platform. Not applause. And certainly not provision. Purpose and obedience to it is what anchors you when everything else is shaking. It matters because if you don't know what you're on this earth for, you'll try to run every time it gets hard—and it will get hard.

Purpose isn't a buzzword. It's not found in a five-step plan or a quick personality test. Ultimately purpose is the will of God, and you don't walk in it until you walk in obedience. Jesus humbled Himself and obeyed, even unto death. Therefore, God exalted Him (see Philippians 2). When Paul wrote of this reality, he was speaking from a place of firsthand experience. From the get-go, he understood that unrelenting obedience would have to be the mode of operation for those following the purpose of the Lord.

But what is purpose? What lies underneath the hood of this thing called purpose? I would argue two things: identity and assignment. We see this playing out clearly in Acts 9 as Pauls' purpose is given to him. He is freshly knocked off his horse and he does not ask for a blessing or for a job. He said two things: "Who are You, Lord?" and "What do You want me to do?" These two simple questions lead to two life-changing foundations in Paul's life: identity and assignment.

The question "Who are You?" establishes who God is and, as a result, who we are. Like father, like son, we cannot know our identity until we know the identity of the One who designed us. The question "What do You want me to do?" is the call to action. It's the next step of obedience that leads Paul on a bread crumb trail of purpose and great exploits for the Lord. This "What shall I do?" posture ought to remain in the pulse of our spiritual lives, not just when we first meet Jesus but during the entirety of our walk with Him.

Everything in my life, from the addiction to the altar, from being a deadbeat dad to a spiritual father to many, has been a road to purpose. I'm not where I am today because I figured it all out. I'm here because I figured out I cannot save nor sustain myself. I am in desperate need of the grace of God to keep me tethered to the will of God. Yes, your purpose comes from God, but so does the power you need to carry it out.

* * *

Not every open door is *your* door to pass through. Sometimes the enemy doesn't show up with a pitchfork; he shows up with a shiny offer that looks like an upgrade. Good salaries. Bigger platforms. Promises of ease. But the Lord didn't call me to ease, He called me to assignment.

You have to be careful, especially when you're tired, not to mistake relief for release. If you're not grounded, a better offer will pull you out of your lane, out of your assignment, and into something that feels good but produces no fruit. I've learned to ask: *Did God open this door, or is it just open?*

The blessing of God doesn't always flow where it's most comfortable; it flows where you're most aligned. I've seen provision pour in, not because we chased after it, but because we stayed faithful to our post. Favor follows obedience. And if you stay rooted where you're sent, God will supply. You don't need every opportunity, you need the *right* one that heaven sends. That's where the oil, growth, and joy is.

While pioneering the ministry, one of the elders at Church on the Rock offered me a full-time ministry position in Florida—a healthy salary, benefits, and private school scholarships for the kids. This was at the time when we weren't even getting paid. On the surface it would've solved a lot of headaches for us. But after praying it through, I told him through tears, "I'm under authority. If you tell me to go, I will. But I know I've heard from God. And if I leave, I'll be disobeying Him."

He slapped the table and said, "Well, what am I supposed to do with that!?"

He understood that I was leading CareCenter, not because an opportunity fell into my lap but because God had intentionally placed me at the helm. Truth is, once you've heard from God, you better get dogged, steadfast, and unmoving. It's more than clever vision statements. We need people who stay planted. People who are willing to die so that something holy can live.

This transcends the "live your best life now" genre of books that exist in the church world. It goes beyond a quick blessing or shallow theology that flatters the flesh. Of course, I believe deeply in the blessing of the Lord. What I'm getting at is the fact that we cannot *abandon* our overarching purpose for the sake of ease.

That sense of unwavering purpose is why I've always connected with apostolic language and function. The word *apostle* was a Roman term originally meaning "sent one." Caesar would send emissaries, usually battle-tested generals, ahead to announce his coming reign. You better believe that these emissaries were keenly aware of their sense of duty, and they also understood the hazards of veering from it. As *sent ones* for the Lord, we've got to maintain a *constant* awareness of purpose.

Think of it like driving a truck loaded with live cargo...you cannot check out for a second. One bump, one wrong turn, and the whole load shifts. Staying in alignment with your calling is the same way. You've got to stay alert, stay yielded, and keep your eyes on where you've been sent and why you've been sent there. One degree off over time and you'll find yourself somewhere you were never intended to be.

I think of David and the trajectory of his life and his steadfast commitment to the purpose of the Lord. David didn't step onto the battlefield against Goliath with an impressive list of credentials. He showed up delivering cheese sandwiches. But he was ready, no less. He'd fought lions and bears in secret. So when the moment came to slay a giant in public, he didn't flinch. *Purpose* had trained him quietly that big, scary beasts aren't so scary in the shadow of his Lord.

The giant-slaying, risk-taking, mountain-moving kind of faith has gripped me since the very beginning of my walk. I had the privilege of witnessing a resurrection as a child. God knew then where my call would lead me and the kind of faith I'd need to live it. We've lived on the edge of faith— trusting God when the math didn't work and when the doors

we thought would open did not budge. Living this way caus-
es onlookers to scratch their heads now and then. In fact, I
would say that if your lifestyle does not occasionally confuse
the crowd, you might want to reevaluate it. Truth is, when
you've surrendered in obedience to a word, there's not a single thing you won't believe God for. Paul wrote, "So then faith
comes by hearing, and hearing by the word of God" (Romans
10:17). And through every battle, every opposition, every
mountain and valley, God has been faithful and on time. *Every* time.

It was a sense of purpose that kept us moving in the
1980s, and it is the purpose that keeps us moving still to this
day. Purpose does more than keep you moving—it keeps you
filtered. A guiding purpose works like a strainer or a net. It
lets the unnecessary fall through while holding onto what's
essential. When you know your assignment, you stop chas-
ing everything that looks good and start holding fast to what
God actually called you to do. That clarity will keep you
when compromise tries to dress up like provision.

One particular story spells that out well.

When the new millennium rolled around, I had been at
the helm of the ministry for almost a decade, and by then, I
needed some time off. I was emotionally drained and physically sick, so I stepped back for a season to get some rest and

treatment for Hep C. I brought in a guy to help—a sharp, corporate type. The sacrifice for the organization was considerable. He wanted $120,000 per year (Jean and I were only making $50,000) but we agreed. It was very much a faith-hire, trusting God to keep things afloat and that the sacrifice would be worthwhile.

While I was out, he began leaning into temp labor contracts with our residents—working stadiums like the American Airlines Arena, the Texas Motor Speedway, and the Ballpark in Arlington. It brought in money—and quite a hefty chunk of it. By the numbers, those jobs grew and eventually made up 41 percent of our operational budget. Beyond the lawn business, this provided guys experience in a fast-paced environment and a new setting.

But over time, something started bothering me.

We were pulling men out of addiction, out of party culture—and now we were putting them right back into environments with booze, scantly-clad women, and concerts. And the people they worked under? They didn't see them as children of God, to put it mildly. They saw them as disposable labor. The message we were trying to teach—*you're the head and not the tail*—was being undercut by the way they were being treated with every event.

It also started to throw our discipleship rhythm out of

whack. The structure, the training, the heart, the timing—it was all getting diluted. I knew God was dealing with me about it, so I approached the board and told them my concerns. Their response was always the same: "We just have to find a way to replace the 41 percent first."

Two years went by. My soul never was settled on the matter. Then contract renewal time came. I sat in that meeting and said, "Listen, I'm in direct disobedience to God if I sign this again. I can't do it. I won't."

That day, I walked away from 41 percent of our operating budget.

No backup plan. No rich donor waiting in the wings. Just a word and a walk.

And over the next few months, miracles started breaking out. Things that were unprecedented. Money came in from unexpected places. Needs were met. A big reserve fund began to form (something we had never had) even after paying our expenses. God didn't just sustain us through the hit, He provided in such a mighty way that we were in a *better* spot financially than before we left the temp labor gigs.

When you align with the voice of God, *you don't lose*—even when it looks like you're giving something up.

Let me make it clear: what facilitated this was not just a moment of courage but a relational infrastructure that has undergirded CareCenter since the start. Many churches and ministries think money is their biggest problem. But it's relationships that's the issue, not money.

It's been said that money follows a mission, but don't forget that mission is carried by *people*. Some ministries are praying for funding but haven't built trust. Others expect folks to sow when they haven't planted anything themselves. And let's be honest, some don't even operate with integrity in how they handle what they do receive.

I don't fall on the legalistic side of tithing, but I believe in tithing as a principle inspired by new covenant, love-based generosity. And a commitment to that generosity usually goes beyond 10 percent when your heart is really in it. We've had grant writers, fundraisers, banquets—all good and necessary things. But those efforts only work long-term when you've got deep relational capital with those around you. When people come into your garden to sow seed, you better be ready to know their name, show gratitude, be transparent, and honor the connection that God has put before you.

Needless to say, we don't chase money—that sort of thing pulls us out of our lanes. I've learned to stay obedient, keep my head down, and let God send the rams into the thicket. When you're where He told you to be, and you are connected to those He sends to you, the incoming provision is non-negotiable. Your job is to simply get up and get ready, no matter the perceived cost.

That's the order of the Kingdom, purpose before provision. Always. When you know your assignment, and you refuse to veer off it for comfort or applause, God makes sure you've got what you need to finish strong. I've lived long enough to see it over and over: the provision shows up when the purpose is settled. If you chase money, you'll end up off-mission. But if you chase obedience, you'll find yourself right in the middle of God's will—with every resource, every relationship, and every open door coming exactly when it's needed. Purpose keeps you planted. Provision just follows the roots.

CHAPTER SEVEN

Fathers and Sons

I've spent much of my life looking both directions—up my bloodline and down it. In both directions, I see a trail of bruises and glory, woundings and wonder, callings answered and callings abandoned. You can't look at fathers and sons throughout biblical and modern history without seeing a mixture of brokenness and redemption. It's tattooed upon the skin of the story.

Some men pick up where their fathers left off; others rebuild the mess their dad left behind. There's something beautiful in the generational tension—the Bible is full of it. Abraham and Isaac, Isaac and Jacob, Elijah and Elisha, David and Solomon, Paul and Timothy. In every one of those stories, there's a moment of transfer. Not just inheritance, but impartation. There's pain in the handoff, and glory too. Sons carry the weight of their father's name, but they also get the chance to redeem it, if need be.

When I look back, I see a line of men who didn't know how to stay. Men who ran, drank, lied, broke things. But I also see moments of brilliance. Talent. Grit. Even a whisper of calling. I see my father, a man I barely knew, yet whose name still shaped mine. And when I look forward, I see my boys. I see spiritual sons and biological ones. I see the burden and blessing of trying to give them something I never had—a father who didn't quit.

Truth is, you don't become a father because you had a child. You become a father when you decide to carry something bigger than yourself, for the sake of someone else. I know the story of the son who ran, and the story of the son who came home. I have resented the line I came from, and I've grown into loving it as well. Because the story of fathers and sons isn't just about where you come from, it's about who you choose to become and what you're willing to embrace when the road turns back toward home.

Lonnie, my oldest among the ones I've raised, had always been sweet-natured, but there was a wild streak in him—this way of thinking that pushed against every line. Tensions grew as he came of age, and by his late teen years, he pretty well rejected my authority all together.

He was seventeen when he left. His mama, just out of prison after ten years, had reentered the picture. I'd worked hard to protect the kids from her, not out of bitterness, but because of her brokenness. She had a history of promising things she couldn't follow through on. But when Lonnie left to go live with her, he didn't last long.

Four months later, he ran into a bank with his buddies and was arrested for armed robbery.

And just like that, he was locked up for ten years.

I blamed myself in part. I had tried to protect him but didn't know how. Thoughts swirled. *Had I driven him into rebellion? Rather than discipline him into manhood?*

I knew how to lead an altar call, but was my own home slipping? Lonnie did ten years and for that decade, I never stopped praying. His name was in my mouth before the Lord on a continual basis. When he finally got out, he didn't reach out to me with a call or connection. He wanted nothing to do with me, and if I'm honest, it tore me up inside. I carried a hope that maybe we'd reconnect once he was free, but it didn't happen and I couldn't force it. All I could do was keep praying.

Then one day, I was on a trip with my son Caleb in Memphis. We had stopped at a Starbucks to get coffee, and after snagging our drinks, we stepped out into the alley behind the store and saw a man sitting on the ground with a card-board sign. The moment I looked at him, something in my spirit stirred. I didn't know why, but I knew I needed to stop.

We got to talking. Turns out he used to be a minister—a nationally known prophet in the Church of God In Christ. He had once walked in real prophetic authority, but he'd fallen hard. Alcohol, relapse, shame. He'd try to clean up and go back into ministry, and it would all come crashing down again.

We sat there and cried together as we talked. Then I felt the Lord whisper, "Give him twenty dollars."

Now listen: that goes against everything in me. I don't hand cash to folks with addiction issues. Funding addiction is not my line of work. But I couldn't shake the instruction, so I handed him the twenty.

He stopped, looked me dead in the eye, and said, "There's something you've been contending for—for ten years. The Lord says this act of obedience is what will bring it to pass."

That was a Saturday.

Tuesday, I got a call.

"Dad . . . can I come home?"

It was Lonnie.

He not only came back into my life but joined me in the ministry at CareCenter and plugged in at Hilltop Church, serving as a pastor for an extended season. He completed Bible school, got his bachelor's degree, married a girl that had come through our women's home, and gave Jean and I three very precious grandchildren. The redemptive arch in my family went beyond this, though. It had been nearly 26 years since losing my children to the state. My son, Eldred Lloyd Sawyer Jr., was just 18 months old when his adoption occurred, which was sealed. His name changed, and for decades I had no clue where he was.

Then one day, out of nowhere, my daughter Meredith was able to track him down. Through a series of circumstances that can only be described as a miracle, we found him. His name was now Douglas Garrett—he'd been adopted into a family that he never quite fit with. His sister was adopted into the same family and adjusted well, but Jr. always seemed out of place. Dark hair, dark eyes—he looked like his mama. They put him in a boys' home, where he was abused, when he was just 14. By the time I found him, he was angry, guarded, and wounded by life.

I went to the apartment where he was living. He was obviously under the influence of meth. When I told him I was his dad, he didn't believe me. He thought I was a cop and started acting out, yelling. I settled him and said, "Just let me tell you a story. Not for me—for you. If you never want to hear from me again after this, I'll respect that."

He calmed down and I told him about the crooked attorneys, the sealed papers, how we were tricked into losing our rights decades earlier. I told him about the years I'd spent wondering, praying, hoping. Somewhere in the middle of it, his walls broke down and tears ran down his face. He stood up, walked over, and embraced me as my arms were stretched wide. From that day forward, we never spoke a harsh word to each other. He never fully came to Christ, though I prayed and tried more than once. Then, after 15 years of reconnection and time together, he tragically took his own life.

When I got the call, there was grief, to be sure, but also a strange kind of gratitude. I was never supposed to see him again. But God gave me 15 years back with my boy. I would never embrace his adopted name, but simply referred to him as Jr. and he respected that. Fifteen holidays. Fifteen birthdays. Fifteen years of catching up. And when the time came, I stood behind the pulpit and preached my own son's funeral.

It wasn't the ending I wanted. But it was more than I had ever hoped for considering how things had begun. In a story marked by loss and brokenness, God still gave me a chapter I didn't deserve, but deeply needed.

* * *

You can live much of your life trying to fix something you don't have the toolkit for. That was me, a father leading sons, still bleeding from my own father wound and the wounds my sin had caused. I knew the ache, but I hadn't named it. And then one day, while reading John 17, Jesus said something that unlocked everything.

Christ was praying during His deepest hour of need before His arrest and crucifixion. He uttered a very simple phrase, "O righteous Father . . ." Those words are about as simple as it gets but struck me like lightning.

Righteous Father.

Growing up, those two words simply did not pair well. However, in a moment, I saw it in John 17: I *did* have a perfect Father. Not just holy and high, but present. Constant. Righteous in every way. In a moment I saw all the ways He had protected and provided for me all my life. The times I should've been dead. Overdoses, accidents, misfiring guns that were intended to kill. The times I had the impression to leave places or get away from certain people. Things that could only be explained as His righteous hand and love preserving me. A Father who never left, never lied, never lashed out. I had read those words before, but on that particular occasion, they didn't just pass through my eyes and mind, but they landed in my spirit. The Lord didn't just father the world, He fathered me specifically, individually.

That moment changed me. It reframed my pain. I remember thinking, *What if I had seen that when I was 6 instead of 36? Would I have stayed out of jail? Would I have raised my kids with more gentleness? Would I have loved my wife more purely?*

There's no use spinning in those questions now. In His righteous sovereignty, He had used it all. But what that revelation gave me was resolve: My sons—spiritual or biological—will not go through life without a father. I tell the men I disciple, "It's easy to be a baby daddy. Being a father is something different." A father is summed up in the word *responsible*. Responsible for providing and protecting, yes physically, but beyond that, he invests in the soul; speaks identity, blessing, and affirmation; and brings correction without crushing. It's not just physical provision; it's emotional presence, spiritual covering, and impartation.

Paul spoke to fatherhood, writing, "For though you might have ten thousand instructors in Christ, yet you do not have many fathers; for in Christ Jesus I have begotten you through the gospel" (1 Corinthians 4:15). In the Greek, the word for *instructors* refers to someone who trains a boy how to behave, like a temporary tutor. But it takes a *father* to show how to become a man. And that kind of fathering? It's not taught. It's caught. The affirmation of the father's heart is spiritual. It's a mantle that rests on you when someone looks you in the eye and says, "I see you. I believe in you. I'll walk with you."

Most cultures around the world have some kind of rite

of passage—something that marks the shift from boy to man. Bar mitzvahs. Tribal ceremonies. Rituals handed down through generations. But here in the West, especially in the church, we've all but lost it. And we may be paying a price as a result.

I didn't get a rite of passage, but what I did get, later in life, was healing. And from that place of healing—from finally knowing I had a perfect Father in heaven—I was able to look back at my earthly father with different eyes. I could finally see him properly. Not just for what he wasn't, but for who he might've been underneath it all. I saw his pain, his brokenness, and even the shame he felt because he couldn't stand in his place.

That's when the Lord started opening a door I never anticipated. I was in my forties when I finally found my father's family. It started in the most unexpected way: with a conversation in a boxing gym, of all places. I'd taken Lonnie to train; he was a gifted and successful Golden Gloves boxer. One of the guys there, a police sergeant who oversaw identification, pulled me aside and said, "Would you be interested in finding your dad?"

"Yeah," I said, "I would."

"Want me to see what I can dig up?"

"Sure."

I gave him my dad's full name and birthplace—Edenton, North Carolina. A few days later, he came back with four potential matches. I called the first one. The man answered and said, "I'm not your dad, but I knew him." Apparently he shared my father's exact name and lived in that area of North Carolina. He then went on to tell me, "I'm sorry to say this, but your father passed away." My heart sank a little as the man added, "I'm actually friends with your uncle. You want his number?"

I did, of course, and that next phone call led to a trip to North Carolina on my 43rd birthday, where I walked into a room full of people I'd never met—aunts, uncles, cousins. All strangers, but somehow it felt like I'd known them all my life.

Most of the folks on my paternal side were around Elizabeth City close to the coast in North Carolina, with some sprinkled around outer banks, just a stone's throw from Kitty Hawk, where the Wright Brothers first flew. I saw old black and white pictures of grandparents and great-grandparents, grainy and tattered, all of them establishing the Sawyer name for generations in that region.

Then my pictures came out. What floored me was this: they all had baby pictures of me and every single one of those photos had one word written on the back: "Hardrock."

It was the name I had resented my entire life, and this whole side of the family knew me by it.

During the trip, my relatives reminisced and told enough stories to fill a book. I learned about my dad's parents, who married very young and were married for 68 years. The story goes that she was at the store when she found out that her husband was hospitalized. When she arrived, he had died, and when the news hit her, she grabbed her heart and died on the spot. They had a double funeral and shut the whole town down for it.

I heard new stories and some old ones about my own father. My uncle told me that my dad came around to have breakfast with his parents one day. Afterward, they had coffee on the porch. He tossed his last swallow of cold coffee from his cup and said, "I'm gonna go get some more coffee." He walked to his red Cadillac convertible and drove off. No one saw him again for 13 years.

What makes a man do that?

I don't know, but I've wrestled with that question most of my life. The story brought a sense of compassion and closure for me, knowing that him leaving me was not just a one-off offense but a pattern of flightiness that plagued my father throughout his life. He didn't just leave me, he left *everyone*.

They told me my dad had gotten saved a year before I did

in the 1980s. Apparently he confessed to his abandonment, got pastoral counseling, and prayed for me every day. In fact, during my trip I sat in the same church seat where he got saved. While I missed him in this life, I'll catch up with him in the next.

There in North Carolina I met a local preacher who knew my dad and asked me to speak in his church, which I gladly took him up on. After I finished the message, he pulled me aside, weeping. He said, "These tears are because your daddy had the call of God on his life. But he ran from it. Seeing you walking in that same mantle has wrecked me."

I left that trip with my heart both full and heavy. It gave me something I didn't even know I needed: closure and connection. I saw where I came from. I saw what could've been. But more importantly, I saw what God had done in spite of it all. The visit didn't rewrite the past, but it reframed it. Since then I've remained in connection with my newfound family in North Carolina. Some of them moved, some of them have passed on, and others remain as they were.

Some time after I met my dad's side of the family, I was gearing up for a motorcycle outreach. I'd started riding with a group that did ministry on two wheels—biker Bible studies, street prayer, real gritty stuff that I am all about.

I'd ridden across the country by then—some of the most

scenic highways in America—and I loved the ministry that came with it. Once a breakdown caused a delay in Wyoming for repairs. The Lord allowed me to present the gospel, lead the man that was doing the work and his family to the Lord, and baptize them in a creek that ran through their property.

One night before a ride, the question came up like it always does in those circles: "What's your road name?" I had been all over on my motorcycle but never once stopped to think about what name I'd carry on my vest.

I knew it couldn't just be something that sounded good. It had to mean something. It had to speak to survival, to grace and grit. It had to capture the truth that I didn't just make it through—I got up when life tried to bury me. It was time to wear the name my father gave me, realizing it was his way of saying he couldn't stay but he had confidence I could be okay. In a way, it was his blessing. It was the name he gave me, and the name my Father in Heaven redeemed: *Hardrock*.

CHAPTER EIGHT

Shifts and Stretches

I f the early years were about surviving, the early 2000s were about stretching. We were outgrowing buildings, budgets, and our own expectations. God wasn't just sustaining the ministry, He was multiplying it. Yes, it was a time of healing in my own family, of reconnection with relatives and deepening roots. But it was also a time of upgrades and expansion in my capacity and spiritual authority. In 2001, we sold our personal home and acquired 12 acres about 50 miles east of Dallas.

We established a home out there, added a barn and a bunkhouse, and brought in eight guys while we still had our men's home operating in Dallas. This property also had the added benefit of creating a good healthy distance between our personal lives and the day-to-day flow of the ministry headquarters, which I had not experienced since stepping into my role.

Some time after, 10 more acres adjacent to us opened up, and we grabbed it. That's where we built a full-scale men's home with accommodations for 30 guys comfortably and 50 if we had to. Out there, the guys worked the land—livestock, chickens, goats, horses, gardens, geese, dogs, you name it. There are so many discipleship lessons found in a garden alone. You can teach a man about patience, process, sowing, and reaping just by handing him a rake and a packet of seeds.

Watching city guys try to trim a goat hoof is something to behold. Many of these men come in at age 35 but with little to no resourcefulness, particularly when it comes to rural work. I've met a number of young men who were as soft as a baby's skin and allergic to discipline. But this atmosphere works something into them. The country slows them down and teaches dignity and hard work.

Back in the city, things were shifting. By 2005, East Dallas was gentrifying fast. The area around our headquarters— our old horseshoe-shaped campus donated in 1990—was no longer poor. Our call had always been to the poor and broken, but here we had seen the community around us transformed. So after two church splits that had replanted in our area, and rising real estate values, we knew it was time to move. The harvest had shifted, so we did too. We sold the donated Eastside property for $700,000 and turned our attention back to Pleasant Grove—my old stomping grounds, still steeped in poverty.

A year before we moved, we sent out intercessors with grid maps and anointing oil. They prayed over every street, every building, every home in our targeted Pleasant Grove zip code, declaring the promises of God over the land. It was spiritual ground-clearing. We were paving the way before a single box was packed.

Not long after, a storefront opened up in a strip mall in Pleasant Grove. I pulled into the parking lot, and I'm not kidding, a tumbleweed rolled across the pavement (we don't usually see tumbleweeds in Dallas). The Lord had given me a word from Isaiah 41:17–20 for the region:

"The poor and needy seek water, but there is none,
Their tongues fail for thirst.
I, the LORD, will hear them;
I, the God of Israel, will not forsake them.
I will open rivers in desolate heights,
And fountains in the midst of the valleys;

I will make the wilderness a pool of water,

And the dry land springs of water.

I will plant in the wilderness the cedar and the acacia tree,

The myrtle and the oil tree;

I will set in the desert the cypress tree and the pine

And the box tree together,

That they may see and know,

And consider and understand together,

That the hand of the LORD has done this,

And the Holy One of Israel has created it."

One interesting point from this passage is, "I will set in the desert the cypress tree." As I researched these statements, I learned a cypress tree requires 150 gallons of water a day to survive. In the desert, that is definitely a supernatural provision that only God can get the glory for.

The building looked half-forgotten, but it had potential.

I called the landlord and told him I was a pastor and wanted to rent the space.

He said, "We don't rent to churches."

"Why not?" I asked.

"Because every preacher thinks God's gonna walk into my office and pay the rent," he said.

He didn't budge.

The next day, I called back and said, "Sir, if you don't want to hear from me again, I'll respect that. But first, let me apologize for every preacher who didn't pay their bills. I get your frustration. Let me assure you, they don't represent me, and they sure don't represent my Lord. If you'll give me a shot, I'll change your mind about churches."

Twenty-four hours later, he called me back.

"Eldred, I'll give you a chance. More than that—I'll cut you a heavily reduced rate."

We moved in fast, cleaned it up, and got to work. Prayer meetings, food pantry, worship services. People came in one way and left another. The presence of God filled that space. Miracles broke out. Christ was glorified.

But nothing in ministry stays still for long. A couple years later, I got a visit from a man named Keith, the CFO of Vista Property Company, which was the firm that had recently bought the shopping center. He walked in with what I later found out was a lockout notice. The look on his face said he meant business. But before he handed the notice to me, something shifted. He looked around and watched what we were doing: feeding the hungry through the basket food pantry that day, and using the men and women from our homes to do the work and pray for the crowds. He slid that envelope back in his pocket and walked out.

Later, he told the property owner, Syd Hurley—a man

who would become one of the most important partners in my life—"If we put those people on the street, our whole project is doomed."

Weeks later, Syd called: not with a lockout notice, but with solutions. He helped us find new space, participated in financial support, and helped fund renovations, eventually joining our board of directors, where he still serves today. He helped us acquire our main campus on Antoinette Street in 2010, which became multi-functional: church sanctuary, gymnasium, community center, and food pantry. We added a Phase 2 home nearby, for guys who hit that fork in the road at six months: ministry track or marketplace track. Those who choose the marketplace learned to pay rent, manage time and money, and maintain healthy relationships. Those who onboarded with the ministry track were raised up for their particular calling in the gospel. That Phase 2 home was donated by Mark Robison, Gus Antos, and Milestone Electric. Mark also joined our board and has helped us tremendously with HVAC and electrical through the years along with generous financial support. Around the same time, we purchased our women's home with a generous gift from someone else. All of it just a short distance from our ministry base.

I used to wonder how the transition would affect the ministry—whether moving out of East Dallas would cost us momentum. But it did the opposite. The church grew during the transition and the outreach multiplied.

Because that's how God works.

He takes tumbleweeds and dead-end lots and turns them into hubs of hope. He flips "we don't rent to churches" into "how can we help?"

He uses men carrying lockout notices to connect dots that form lifelong partnerships. He opens doors we couldn't budge and funds projects we didn't even pray for. That building wasn't just a place to meet. It was a sign of what happens when you keep obeying, one day at a time.

Growth doesn't come without stretching, though. Multiplication carries a cost.

Between acquiring properties, managing building projects, running a growing church, launching new homes, preaching, discipling, and answering calls at all hours—I was juggling more than any two people should have. And the crazy thing is, I flourished in it. Not because I had the strength, but because the pressure drove me head first into the grace of God.

We were launching a men's home during the crack epidemic in the '80s, planting food pantries in some of the poorest communities in the nation, vetting referrals manually, underwriting housing projects, and trying to keep up with everything the Spirit was stirring.

Many folks didn't get it. I've always been wired differently and tended to flourish when the pile was high and the pressure was on. My brother Austin used to say, "Don't worry about the mule, just load the wagon." Why? Because it keeps me humble. It keeps me leaning on the Lord when things are stacked up. There were weeks when I was never fully off the clock, phone always buzzing, crisis always one call away. There were times I would bottom out, feeling like I couldn't catch a break and desperately needed a win. I'd get on the tractor out at the property with just me, the land, and God, and I'd cry. I'd reached the end of myself for the millionth time and in that quiet, He'd whisper, "I love you." Even when I felt useless and spent, I could count on the Lord's tender affirmation.

* * *

Being the mule that pulls the overloaded wagon isn't for everyone. In reality I had been prepared to carry sizable burdens for years. In fact, I was still green as ever when the Lord first whispered it to me.

It was 1988. I was in prayer, just learning how to hear the voice of God clearly, when I heard it deep in my spirit: "I am preparing you as an apostle to the poor."

I didn't run out shouting it. I had read enough of the New

Testament to know that being called an apostle to the poor was not something to get excited about. It's not a title, it's a weight. And back then, I wasn't even sure what to do with it. So I sat on it, telling no one.

Years later, in the early '90s, Terry Moore came to me and said, "Eldred, you carry an apostolic gift for this region." It was confirmation—but also a sign that the time for sitting on it was nearing its end. And sure enough, as we began the move into Pleasant Grove around 2007, over a decade after Pastor Terry's confirmation, something shifted. Not just around me, but in me. It was like I stepped into something I'd been carrying for years without knowing how to wear it. The apostolic mantle landed fully, and I began to operate in a new level of clarity, authority, and multiplication.

The apostolic gift isn't about hierarchy, it's about function.

It means you wear different hats in different seasons—evangelist, teacher, pastor, prophet, business manager, board chair—whatever the moment calls for. It's about being sent to a specific region and building what God assigns, with a blueprint and authority to do so. And in 2007, as I hit my 20th year in ministry, the Lord spoke again: "You've been faithful with what belongs to another, Leonard's vision. Now I'm giving you your own."

From that moment on, the fathering, building, and multiplying graces on my life became unmistakable. In fact, the years between 2007 and 2010 were soaked in the presence of God in a very unique way. We saw unprecedented favor, growth, and miracles. Not just in our sanctuary, but everywhere our people set foot. It was like the kingdom spilled out of the walls and started claiming territory wherever we stepped within our assigned region.

I'll never forget walking into a National Tire and Battery one day. I was standing at the counter when a woman behind the register gave me a strange look. She grabbed her chest, her head dropped back, and she collapsed. No breathing. No pulse. She was gone.

There were panicked women standing nearby and I said, "I don't know if y'all know how to pray, but I'm gonna pray in the Holy Ghost. If you know how to pray in tongues, go for it. If not, pray in your understanding."

I put my hand on her head and commanded life to come back into her, just like I'd witnessed my grandmother do as a boy. Within seconds, she came to. Breath entered her lungs and life came back in her dead eyes. By the time the ambulance arrived, she was sitting up, and when I came back later and asked the manager about her, he said, "She came back later to get her car and the doctors gave her a clean bill of health. No issues."

And it didn't stop there.

One of the couples in our church was at a public pool when a child drowned. They ran over, laid hands on him, and prayed, and the child was raised from the dead on the spot. Another time, at the American Airlines Center, one of our temp labor teams was working when a woman collapsed. Similarly, she had no heartbeat and no breath. Our guys—just men from the program—laid hands and prayed, and she came back before the paramedics arrived.

We saw a man with advanced cancer get healed—so completely that the doctors were convinced they'd misdiagnosed him, producing a letter stating as much. We saw marriages on the brink come back from the dead, people getting saved left and right. And it wasn't just street addicts. We started seeing white-collar professionals—people with careers, degrees, country club memberships—confessing they'd been battling addiction too. Pills, alcohol, drugs of every kind. The gospel didn't care about your tax bracket, it came for everybody.

We were experiencing the blessings that flowed from the five-fold ministry directive. God established these gifts and offices within the church, saying they are "for the equipping of the saints for the work of ministry, for the edifying of the body of Christ" (Ephesians 4:12).

Clergy does not do ministry for the laity. Clergy equips the laity for the ministry. In so doing, faith breeds faith. When people start seeing miracles, they stop asking "if" and start asking "who's next?"

That's the apostolic anointing—not just to believe, but to build environments where others begin to believe too. It's about more than miracles. It's about multiplication. Apostolic calling doesn't just raise up followers, it raises up sons. Paul said in 1 Corinthians 4:15, "For though you might have ten thousand instructors in Christ, yet you do not have many fathers." Instructors can teach you how to do something, but fathers impart who they are.

Fathers don't just hand out tasks, they hand down identity. They build on sons, not on strangers and hirelings. That's why Paul said to Timothy, "You therefore, my son, be strong in the grace that is in Christ Jesus. And the things that you have heard from me . . . commit these to faithful men who will be able to teach others also" (2 Timothy 2:1–2). That's legacy and apostolic DNA. You pour it in and get down low in the dirt with them so they can pour it forward. And when the building is on sons—not hired hands—it stands when the storm hits.

But not every ministry out there is building like that.

There are men today who call themselves spiritual fathers, but what they're really doing is identifying gifts they can use for the promotion of their ministry. They'll point to a young man and say, "He can build something. Let's send him out," but the motive's all wrong. It's not about developing people, it's about leveraging them. I have sons I've invested in for years who have left our network, changed their ministry names, and adapted their model to meet the needs of the communities they serve with no financial support back to me or our ministry. I can readily rejoice with them and for them as they take what I've imparted and built on it. No matter the direction or models they create to be who they are, where they are, the DNA of the one who raised them up and sent them will be present. Other models we often see are not fathering—that's farming for profit. Oh, and trust me, this is something I've had to learn by trial and error, after following popular models of apostolic hierarchy. Call me a realist (some would say cynical), but I've seen too much to be naive. I've watched platforms rise without roots. I've watched gifting get exalted above character.

I was once invited to speak at a pastors conference to share our "model" of ministry. I declined, telling them, "I don't think it would be fair." Because we don't recruit a team of mature volunteers and slot them into a polished system. We build from the ground up. From scratch. With broken, crushed, addicted people who come in with nothing to lose but baggage. And we see them developed with character and purpose, being prepared to fulfill their part in God's story, written before the foundation of the world.

It's not as though we select from a pool of mature, seasoned leaders and Christians and fit them into a job description that fits their aptitude, personality, and spiritual gift test. Our leadership model is to build on sons who've adopted our heartbeat. And these are truths that can't really be shared and applied in a tidy seminar.

And this unique edge might also be why I rub some people the wrong way at times. I've heard that folks either love me or hate me—without much middle ground. I've been labeled overbearing or too intense at times. And maybe I am. I've often said, rarely does a soldier leave boot camp loving his drill instructor, but after surviving a few fire fights, winning some real battles, and taking some legitimate ground, their perspective and appreciation begins to shift. I've had many men leave here angry, only to come back later expressing gratitude. I certainly don't have a messiah complex. But I do know this: Jesus had a similar effect during the course of His ministry.

The truth is, I believe we're smack dab in the middle of a delusion in the church. Paul wrote in 2 Thessalonians that because they did not love the truth, "God sent them a strong delusion" (see 2:9–11). We are watching a great falling away. And while I'm not a stargazer waiting around for Jesus to come back, I am staying focused on the mission. We've got a job to do. There is urgency; the night cometh. And until He calls me home or tells me otherwise—I'll keep showing up with two hands on the plow.

CHAPTER NINE

Growing Pains

Not every open door is a green light. But some doors, God kicks wide open and nearly shoves you through. That's how we found ourselves multiplying beyond Texas. What started as one men's home in the middle of Dallas turned into a network of locations across five different states. And what's even more remarkable is this: every one of them is led by men who started just like I did—addicted, broken, behind bars, or barely holding on. They were men with nothing but a yielded heart and the call of God on their life. They emerged ready to build.

The first launch happened almost by accident in our eyes, but very purposeful in the Lord's. It was 2012. I sold off some cows and decided to take the family on a vacation to get away and reset. We booked a spot on the White River near Cotter, Arkansas. But what we got was anything but peaceful. Medical issues, family tension, and an RV park in the front yard of what was advertised as a secluded cabin—we wound up calling it "the vacation from hell." Nevertheless, I figured out a long time ago that sometimes these scenarios are just labor pains and God prepping a miracle.

That Sunday, we were hunting for a church to visit. We drove around a bit until I spotted one. I felt a pull to go in. Turns out there was a man attending who'd just been released from jail the day before and was already playing the pastor like a fiddle. I had seen it before and knew the game. I introduced myself to the pastor and said, "If you want, I can help you out with that guy." I did and the guy left.

I proceeded to tell him what I did and we enjoyed a good 10-minute conversation. Later during the service, the pastor invited me to share about our ministry. As I spoke, I noticed a couple in the congregation weeping. *It was Father's Day.* Afterward, the man could barely get a word out, he was so wrecked. They came up after service and told me about their son—addiction, jail, in and out. We prayed right there. And I knew as we prayed: this wasn't a random moment. It was a setup.

I handed the man a card and said, "When your son comes home—and he will—call me."

We were in Cotter, Arkansas. The family's legacy ran deep in the town. Their ancestor had once ridden three days home on his horse after finishing a job, only to realize he'd been overpaid. So he turned around and rode three days back to return the money. The act of integrity became so legendary that they named the town's bridge after him.

Needless to say, their prodigal son came from a long line of integrity and high standards. But the enemy had ensnared him, and he couldn't walk in it.

Eventually, just as I told them, their son came home and got right. They called me and he came into our program where he grew quickly. When his time was up, he knew God was calling him back to Arkansas. We sent him—fully equipped and covered to establish an extension of our ministry in his home town. From day one, it exploded. They saw expansion, donated vans, property, and a huge community response. At the first banquet we hosted, people showed up just to hear his story. That's what happens when the DNA of the house goes with the man. We take the people who had been destroying the community and send them back in to serve that community, hands on.

When we send guys out, we always start with the men's home first because that's a labor force and army of gospel soldiers, much like the original salvation army. Just like our original model in Dallas, these satellites establish a lawn business and other service-related cottage industries, which instantly become a training ground to instill work ethic, dignity, life skills, and revenue. From there, any men who enter the home are taken on a bartering basis where we charge certain amounts for room, board, classes, transportation, meals, and so forth. For six months, guys work at a hypothetical rate per hour and that covers the cost of everything else, so no entry fees, no insurance, come as you are. Just real work, sweat equity, and real structure producing real transformation.

Others built on the same foundations and principles. A son of the house, Daniel Awabdy, who was in addiction for 22 years and looking at a potential habitual enhancement that carries a life sentence, met the man I earlier referred to as Kent when he came to minister in the jail he was in. Kent told him he had gotten his life turned around at CareCenter some 25 years earlier and that he should try and go there. God worked a literal miracle, and Daniel was released to us and transformed through discipleship, teaching him to hear the voice of God. He did just that and heard *CareCenter Jackson Mississippi.* He was trained and sent out to plant where he has labored for years now. It is one of our stand out locations and is making major impact in the city of Jackson, duplicating our model in the inner city there.

We tried opening a home in other places, but they didn't last. We've learned, you can't have the brand without the burden. These plants are not platforms for personal advancement, but for all in sacrifice forging real faith. Beyond that, there is a balance that a leader in this field needs. Some people, for example, are too mercy-driven to do this kind of work. Unfettered mercy without order becomes tolerance, and tolerance becomes chaos. Paul told Titus, as he sent him to the unique culture of Crete, "Set things in order" and raise up leaders from that disorderly culture. You don't get to disciple men without getting your hands dirty—and sometimes that means a stern fatherly rebuke. If you want to set up a shelter, that's one thing. But if you're building an apostolic base, with a vision to multiply, you need backbone. Many people want a therapist, not a pastor. They want to stay stuck on themselves, but the problem is you cannot naval gaze your way into freedom. We teach the cross first, then from that place we find the wholeness, freedom, and purpose we're all looking for. William Booth, the founder of the Salvation Army, was once asked to put his message into one word, he responded, "Others."

Over time I've established a hard line that we only send sons. We don't promote hirelings. A hireling won't walk through the fire with you, and fire is part of the process. Every leader we now send out started in the trenches—serving, scrubbing, submitting. We don't look for the most charismatic guy in the room or the one with the most credentials. We look for the one who's still standing when the fires are down to embers. We build our disciples from a foundation stemming from Luke 16:10–12, *"He who is faithful in what is least is faithful also in much; and he who is unjust in what is least is unjust also in much. Therefore if you have not been faithful in the unrighteous mammon, who will commit to your trust the true riches? And if you have not been faithful in what is another man's, who will give you what is your own?"*

Faithfulness, a healthy fear of God, and a true revelation of the call of God and burden—that leads to a strong commitment that you are set apart from this world's systems. These are the essential foundations required to build on the kind of faith it takes to pioneer and plant a work like ours. That's who you can build on. There are guys leading locations who began by holding a bucket of water and a sponge, washing vehicles.

We formalized the apostolic approach by creating our Academy of Inner-City Missions—AIM, we call it. It's the school where we send the ones who know they are called, training them as missionaries to be sent. We use a reading list for every student in the program—15 books that shape leaders, from *The Making of a Leader* by Frank Damazio to *Master Plan of Evangelism*, by Robert Coleman. We don't just preach it—we train it. We employ a curriculum that earns them an associate's degree in biblical studies, and it uses daily hands-on ministry work and outreach as practicum.

We watch 1 Samuel 10:6 and 2 Corinthians 12:9 manifest in their lives, in spite of them: "Then the Spirit of the LORD will come upon you, and you will prophesy with them and be turned into another man." "And He said to me, 'My grace is sufficient for you, for My strength is made perfect in weakness.' Therefore most gladly I will rather boast in my infirmities, that the power of Christ may rest upon me."

The truth is, too many programs build around recovery. We don't. We build around resurrection. Sobriety isn't the goal, it's a byproduct. When you live in resurrection power, addiction loses its grip. I've seen people leave the world behind only to build an altar to their sobriety. It becomes their new god. But we're not here to make people sober. We're here to facilitate them becoming sons and daughters through the power of the gospel, disciples who make disciples.

That's why we're careful about how we build. We don't move unless there's a burden. All vision begins with burden. Not just an idea—a God-breathed burden. That's how you know it's real. If it keeps you up at night, if it won't let you go, if it breaks your heart before it breaks the ground—you might have something worth building.

And when that moment comes, when the door cracks open and God says, "Go," we don't hesitate. We've learned what to do. We listen. We submit it to wise counsel. We test it with the Word. And then we do what we've always aimed for: obedience.

Because the call isn't just to stay faithful or maintain what we have—it's to multiply. And when He sends us to expand, we do so accordingly. We have more locations on our radar. Many areas are struggling across the country. We carry burdens for different places, but the last thing I want to do is get ahead of God. Because we've chosen to build on sons, we do not have some geographic master plan of franchising the ministry to every county in America. Instead, we allow the organic outflowing of the Spirit to guide our moves as sons and daughters of the house are established and sent. No hirelings. No shortcuts. Just proven people with oil on their lives and a burden that can't be shaken. Because here's the truth—you don't want performance without presence. You don't want entertainment with no glory. And I've lived long enough to know: the enemy doesn't show up with a pitchfork and neon sign saying, "Take a hard left into heresy" or "Mission drift starting *now*." No, he's subtle. He whispers compromises. He lets one generation drift, while the next one sinks. And if we don't pay attention, we'll preach power while living powerless.

So often today, we find pulpiteers with platforms, but we are starving for fathers with presence. We don't need another influencer; we need intercessors standing in the gap. Men who will pour out their lives, raise sons and daughters, and not just deliver sermons but impart truth. It has always been about the death of the will, crucifixion of the flesh, and stubborn obedience to the end. That's what breaks yokes, changes the trajectory of generations, and releases the aroma of heaven. It'll cost you everything, but you still say yes. This is the gospel—it's not a concept. It's power. "For in it the righteousness of God is revealed from faith to faith; as it is written, 'The just shall live by faith'" (Romans 1:17).

There is no kingdom without power. And that's what separates a form of godliness from the real thing. So as we multiply, we aren't just sending organizational leaders taught to repeat mantras. We're sending fire-branded sons and daughters with the DNA of the house, ready to claim regions for Jesus.

"For I am not ashamed of the gospel of Christ, for it is the power of God to salvation for everyone who believes, for the Jew first and also for the Greek. For in it the righteous-

ness of God is revealed from faith to faith; as it is written, 'The just shall live by faith.'" (Romans 1:16-17)

I want to be clear that this is a work of the Holy Spirit, not unique to CareCenter, but it can only be accomplished by the transforming power of the gospel, and it happens in spite of the recipients. No religious structure, system, or formula can accomplish this. And because of this truth, no flesh can glory in it. Our God is a jealous God and He will not share His glory with any man. It is a grace only released to the humble who recognize fully that He is God and we are not.

* * *

Rippling across state lines and having ministry pop off around the country does not come without trouble. With growth comes glory but also grind, problems, and flat out spiritual warfare.

I would be remiss to not mention the realities of warfare and the need for discernment when pioneering a meaningful work for God. It's often the case that when ministry multiplies, so does the possibility of attack. If you're stepping into building a ministry of any kind, you'd better learn to see demonic activity at play—not out of a sense of paranoia, but out of keen discernment.

What does it look like? Sometimes it's obvious. We've

seen people in the parking lot throwing herbs, doing chants to conjure up something against our cause. But the most dangerous attacks often show up subtly, beneath the radar.

My first real exposure came in the early days of the ministry. We had come out of a massive nationwide prayer movement, and behind that victory was a fierce counterattack: occult pressure, covert infiltration, subtle division.

In my first exposure to this stuff, we had a couple come into our midst. They were charismatic and seemingly spiritual, helping in the ministry and plugging in. However, alarm bells sounded early. The lady was seductive in her behavior; her husband was very passive and quiet which brought Jezebel and Ahab to mind.

Before long, we were at their house for a home group when I noticed there was a demonic symbol on the inside of their door jam. I confronted them head on, "You guys are witches, aren't you?"

"We are," she said matter-of-factly.

"And you're on assignment?" I asked.

"Yes."

What's your assignment?"

She said, "Our ministry is division."

Of course, we flushed them out and I learned a valuable truth: if you confront the occult, you can expose it and get rid of it in short order.

Not long after, we received a phone call from a major ministry who said a man had gotten saved on the east coast during one of their crusades and needed to relocate. They figured the change in scenery and demographics at Care-Center would be good for him.

We picked him up from the bus station and brought him in. After being here for just one night, we began getting phone calls from anonymous callers saying, "We know you have him. We're gonna get him."

Of course, I talked to him at length and his salvation was genuine. Turns out, he had been a high ranking priest in the occult. He had been to Haiti where he was involved in human sacrifices and at one point in our conversation, he presented his hand and showed me a scar from a bone he had removed from his body to sacrifice to satan. I spent a few days with him, and he opened up to me with great vulnerability.

I was struck by how well he knew the Scriptures. When I mentioned this he said, "Well, they teach us to know our enemy."

I realized in that moment how much naïveté we tolerate as Christins—thinking that everything around us is so sanitized and safe. He elaborated, "We infiltrate churches all the time. And basically the main mode the occult uses to disrupt churches is *division*." In no uncertain terms he made it clear they did not have to go in and do spells and incantations. They just throw money around. You get people with money in positions of authority and have them undermine the leadership, cause division and blow up the work.

He then added, "We have a goon squad out of California who go looking for defectors like me. You'll start seeing them soon. They drive in Volkswagen beetles with California license plates. They're big muscly guys."

I was skeptical. People may think I'm crazy when I say this but shortly after this, I got another phone call about the man we took in from an unknown number. I then stepped outside and sure enough, across the street was a big guy in sunglasses, leaning against a beetle with California plates just staring at me.

The man we took in disappeared not long after, whether he was kidnapped or went back to the occult, we don't know.

The reality is: there is an intentional effort from an organized occult faction who wants to cause division and destroy the work of God. They do not come in with obvious anti-Christ sentiments, but they come in quoting scripture and sharing testimony. From there, the ranks are climbed, authority is undermined, and disaster unfolds if you don't expose it early.

Over the years, more stories followed. Some I identified

fast, others I failed to spot and expose as quickly as I should have. On one occasion, we had a respected couple come from another church. They cited that their pastor, whom I knew and valued, had sent them.

I had known them from many years before at a major church where they had influence and positions of influence. When it seems as though someone has respect from someone you respect, it's easy to ignore the red flags. Especially in this case because they had come offering money and help at a time when we desperately needed both. In fact, I was intoxicated by the prospect of having mature help and financial support.

Looking back, I should not have been so quick to go along to get along. I would have tested things harder up front. Nevertheless, she began climbing the ladder and eventually counseling people within our congregation—including many of my key leaders. In this private room, she required complete confidentiality which was a major red flag. As you can imagine, eventually it came out that she was undermining me and upending the direction I was leading the ministry completely in these private meetings.

Eventually, their former pastor came out to visit a man he had sent into our men's home. I said to him, "Have you had trouble with *so and so*?"

He immediately began to tear up. "I'm so sorry Eldred."

We got through the apologies and I got to the heart of what I was discerning, "Do you feel it's witchcraft? I'm not talking 'rebellion is as witchcraft'...but do you feel they have an actual assignment for division."

"Absolutely," he said.

Later, we talked for a couple hours and told stories of the division and trouble he'd seen and experienced.

When I exposed the situation for what it was, they packed up, sold their home and moved across the country. They knew I had their number and had figured out the dark mandate. I had seen it before.

Make no mistake: the common denominator in every one of these dark moments has been division. It often begins as a seed in a private room, a whispered "let's pray together," masking what's really being planted. It is the age old practice of "Divide and Conquer". If a kingdom is divided against itself, that kingdom cannot stand. And if a house is divided against itself, that house cannot stand (see Mark 3:24-25).

The opposite is unity. In 2 Chronicles 5, the priests could not stand up due to the weight of the glory cloud. What preceded this? All of the people coming together in unity as a singular voice raised unto the Lord. The Holy Ghost explosion in Acts 2 erupted only when hearts were synchronized.

Unity precedes power. So disruption becomes the natural assignment of darkness—especially over any genuine work of God.

Still: not every opposition is demonic. Some of it is spiritual immaturity, poor boundaries, ignorance. Being juvenile is not the same as being rebellious. Nevertheless, guard your heart, protect your inner circle, test what looks good and don't leap at every invitation.

Be alert. Be sober. Know who you are in Christ—and carry a word for your region. Because when you do, no matter how sharp the claws, no matter how hidden the strategy, no matter how many tentacles try to entangle—you'll find yourself still standing in the light of His grace. We press on, not in the absence of enemy fire, but in the assurance of our King.

CHAPTER TEN

Where Honor Is Due

It was a quiet morning in 2007. I was praying as usual when the Lord spoke clearly to my heart: "You are about to receive a $100,000 gift."

A word like that is enough to send you into a fit of hallelujahs. At the time, we had not received a donation that came close to six-figures. What came next would stretch me in a very public way. God said, "I need you to tell the people about it."

So not only did I receive a private word that we would soon receive a donation bigger than anything we had ever gotten, but I was now required to include the faith required to declare it to the congregation before any evidence was tangible. If I had misheard, it would be made publicly known and fast.

So I did as I was told. That Sunday I stood up and announced, "The Lord spoke to me that we will soon receive a $100,000 donation." The next Sunday came, no 100k, and I made the same announcement—not for show, but to be obedient. Finally, the third Sunday came and my announcement stayed consistent.

And then, on Thursday, the call came from my office manager, voice trembling with excitement. "Are you sitting down? We just received a check for $100,000."

I can't say I was surprised—God did exactly what He said He would do. But I was in awe at His faithfulness and majesty afresh. Those funds came from people who had walked with us back in the 1990s, leading our children's ministry. They'd built a healthcare business and sold it for a healthy return—and God moved their hearts to give.

Why speak it into the room before seeing it in the bank? Because faith is born in spoken words and shared vision—even before the check arrives.

> *"Now faith is the substance of things hoped for, the evidence of things not seen. For by it the elders obtained a good testimony. By faith we understand that the worlds were framed by the word of God, so that the things which are seen were not made of things which are visible."* (Hebrews 11:1–3)

As you've read, things certainly did not start with these sorts of massive influxes. We had gone from praying for rice to stewarding and multiplying substantial gifts on a regular basis. Finances began to flow not because I worked harder—I had been laboring with great effort from the start—but because God built a bridge with the supporting pillars being faith, faithfulness, generosity, serving the community, and dogged obedience resulting in longevity. He began to bring men of means from the suburbs into our inner-city mission. A man from a suburban church, owner of an advertising start-up, began sending small contributions—$20 a month—and engaging his family in inner-city outreach and missions. Over time, his business expanded exponentially and his generosity swelled into a six-figure annual gift. It was more than money; it was a connection of hearts, a shared calling. I learned early that these relationships are mutual: they need us as much as we need them. Our Return on Investment isn't counted in dollar signs. It's in changed lives, restored families, broken generational patterns, and entire neighborhoods revived.

Somewhere along the way, I found myself pastoring these men at some level, many of whom don't attend our church. I have a sincere desire to counsel and connect with them in a way that brings them life. It's not some cheap "sow a seed and I'll send a prayer cloth that heals everybody and grows your business." Instead, it's a heartfelt shepherding that results in a double thank you. The exchange of spiritual and natural resources is the biblical model. The kingdom of God doesn't operate like a slot machine, dropping coins, hoping for a jackpot. It runs on relationships. And when those relationships are forged by the Spirit, the exchange of spiritual and natural resources is a beautiful byproduct. That's not just ministry philosophy. It's the Bible.

In Acts 28, Paul ends up shipwrecked on the island of Malta. He's not there for a revival meeting. He's there by seemingly bad circumstances, but God's always working. Paul prays for the local chief's father, and the man gets healed. Next thing you know, a healing wave sweeps the island. People are being touched, lives changed. And you know what the response was? "Then all the other sick people on the island came and were healed. As a result we were showered with honors, and when the time came to sail, people supplied us with everything we would need for the trip" (Acts 28:9–10 NLT).

That's the model. God moves through His people, and the people respond—not with claps and thank yous, but with real-world provision to fuel the next leg of the journey. "Donor relations," as it's often called, is reciprocal—and it has to be. It is divine connections and shared kingdom agreement. One-sided relationships don't last. When we partner together, everyone invests and brings something to the table. I've learned to communicate in business terms with many of the men in my circle, and they've learned to communicate in ministry terms. While many of them operate corporate structures, they understand our culture and mission field, which is very blue collar. Our two worlds complement the other, giving freedom to us both. I don't suppose I can go into their world and run their businesses, and they understand we have been called to our very different world, and they give us freedom and support without control, supporting our vision.

Of course, none of this springs up in a vacuum. It flows out of the global church of Jesus. Divine confirmation, spiritual authority, pastoral oversight—these weren't optional for me. I've always believed that sending comes from a foundation, and launching only works when there's a voice behind it saying, "Go."

* * *

By 2012, a nagging fear had settled in: what would happen to my wife, Jean Marie, if I fell over dead? Pride and insecurity had crept in, and I began to feel—I'll be honest—entitled.

I had spent decades discipling broken men, not planning and optimizing a 401K. We had no conventional securities. During that season, a business leader I respected invited me into his office, and he asked simply, "What's your debt?" When I shared we owed $125,000 on the house, he immediately wrote a check. No questions. No meetings. The board gave me the donation as a deferred compensation, in part for the ten years that we did not receive a salary. With the brief stroke of a pen, we were out from under the grip of debt.

Then it got better. The CareCenter board began thinking longterm. The question of facilities, successors, and properties came up. The board decided to buy our home from us as a parsonage we could live in at no cost, while affording us a reserve as we stepped into the fourth quarter of our ministry. God secured us—but only after I laid down my fear, my pride, and my expectations. Many naysayers, who didn't understand and called us crazy in the early pioneering years, haven't prospered near as well, with all their hard work.

I'm reminded of the passage in 1 Samuel that states, "Has the LORD as great delight in burnt offerings and sacrifices, As in obeying the voice of the LORD? Behold, to obey is better than sacrifice, And to heed than the fat of rams" (15:22).

The sowing and planting from decades prior was being rewarded and honored with late stage harvests that I could not have predicted or produced on my own. Even down to Jean Marie's vehicle. I mentioned prior that as a single mother, she gave away her car to a lady who needed it so many years before. Well, the guys in our various locations all chipped in and bought her a Nissan Pathfinder—far nicer than the vehicle she gave up all those years before.

Divine appointments have shaped every mile of my journey. We are not flourishing because we planted a ministry on an island, divorced from the greater body of Christ. We are prospering in our golden years of ministry because God is faithful to allow us to partake in the harvest that He is bringing about.

Many years had passed since our days in Church on the Rock, and I stayed somewhat connected with several of the leaders from those days. A deep love and family connection remained. One evening I was at a conference on a Thursday night, and a friend from Church on the Rock and I thought of Pastor Larry Lea, and we began to pray with burden for him. We wondered how he was and what he was up to. It had been 18 years since I'd seen him but had no way to reconnect. That Sunday, an old friend of mine ran into Larry at a meeting, and Larry said, "If you see Eldred, give him my number."

I called him Monday and he said, "Eldred, you won't believe this. I was in a borrowed car. It caught fire and burned up. I was stranded on the side of the highway when an old Church on the Rock member pulled up and drove me to Enterprise. Turns out, they don't have any cars available so I'm stuck."

"I'll be there in 20 minutes," I said.

We walked together for the next three years, and he based out of our church sharing the pulpit with me.

And since that day, we've remained in contact and rekindled a friendship. Loyalty carried across decades and pulled us together once more. Now his prayer message is being followed on a 6 a.m. Zoom call every morning, and it's being taught and applied in our prison ministry. Convicts are being trained and facilitating prayer movements behind the walls of prison. This will ensure this global prayer movement will pass to the next generation.

Beyond Pastor Larry, there are those whose names carry the fragrance of grace and trust in my spirit—people who acted as cornerstones in the building of my testimony. I think of my grandmother, Nanny Bishop, whose fervent prayers lit fires that still burn to this day. I think of Austin, who was imperfect but instilled a sense of work that I did not have until that summer on the job site. He took me under his wing—and even if that wing was broken at times, I'm a better man for my time with him.

My mind lands on Leonard Brannon, who took me in when the rest of the world wouldn't have touched me with a 10-foot pole. The price paid by him and his family to position me to carry this ministry cannot be understated or understood. Unless you were there, you just can't know. He was there at my lowest hour and nurtured me in the faith and the ministry. It's no understatement to say that I would not be where I am today without him. I consider David Wilkerson, whose prophetic voice spoke over me even before I heard it myself. My meeting with him was a hinge that much of my ministry has swung by since.

Then there is Robert Summers, who refused my resignation and spoke words of affirmation that shifted my direction—and solidified my soul. I ponder Terry Moore, who has become my pastor and spiritual covering, who shepherded our family through seasons of transition and provided emotional and practical resources that exceed the generosity of most, and he still stands in that place today, as a spiritual father and covering. I cannot forget Joe and Nancy Martin of Trinity Church, faithful friends who have loved and supported us in the tough seasons and provided financial support from the day they opened their doors.

There's Gene Lewis, who challenged me to tithe off the ministry income when we had nothing, marking the breaking of a poverty spirit off our ministry. I think of Gary Turner, who left me a watch as a prophetic symbol of season and time, and then Charles and Sharon Burton, who married Jean Marie and me, standing with us like spiritual parents as we learned to leave the nest. My board of directors and their families, who have intentionally invested more than required. People like Syd and Elizabeth Hurley, Mark and Sabrina Robison, Gus and Amanda Antos. Chris and Vanessa McCrea, who I love deeply and have watched develop as a spiritual son and successor to my father Terry Moore, ensuring the divine connection will remain into the next generation. Scott and Nancy Hinkle, Heath and Jennifer Hill and their boys, John and Nan Kirchhoffer, and many unmentioned that I can only hope have received back as much as they've sown and more.

There is my dear friend Darren McCarty, an attorney who has become closer than a brother and a true friend in times of need. Then the many people who have served alongside us through the years and in different seasons. One standout is Pastor Melvin Gipson, a man who literally defines faithfulness—who labored with me daily for 25 years in the good, the bad, and the ugly. The men and women who began as recipients in our men's and women's home who have walked with me for decades, becoming pillars in our midst, spiritual mothers and fathers to our people, and family to ours. People like Redell and Crystal Davis, Robert and Barbara Jacubowski, Jeremy and Maria Crane, Mannie and Ocie Jefferson, and more than I can name but you know. I think of our children Lonnie, Meredith, Rebekah, Caleb, Jeri, Naomi, and Dannah, who lived this life without asking for it and have brought more joy than they could have ever known. And—most of all—Jean Marie, my wife, my partner, my soulmate, without whom none of this would have been possible.

These relationships are more than alliances; they are deep, spiritual riverbeds carved out over decades. With each one, I have walked alongside people who gave me direction when I was lost, rebuke when I needed course correction, and grace when I stumbled. I have received love, mercy, challenge, affirmation—and at times, a firm hand of accountability. As I look back on nearly 40 years of "yes"—yes to God, yes to the call—I still shake my head in sheer awe. Had anyone told the young man who fell to his knees that this extraordinary journey awaited him, I would have laughed it off as impossibly grand.

Along the way, I've heard gratitude from others: "Thank you for saying yes." My reflex reply? "My *yes* was more like crying, 'Uncle!'" And when someone thanked me for what's been built here, I'd shrug and say, "It's been built in spite of me—if I could have messed it up, I would have a long time ago."

Every single day of my life carries with it a tempered astonishment. Every testimony shared, every life restored—it's all surpassed even my wildest hopes. And though this is a memoir of God's faithfulness in my life, it has never truly been about me. It's been about honoring those who came before, serving those whose paths were laid before us, and trusting with every ounce of our being in the One who made it all possible.

And so I harbor a deep gratitude for every soul who poured into me, for every miracle God made happen, every divine connection, every resource given when it seemed impossible—and for the cascade of grace that continues to this very moment, *in spite of me.*

"God sets the solitary in families; He brings out those who are bound into prosperity; but the rebellious dwell in a dry land." (Psalm 68:6)

Me with Mom & Dad before he left

Nanny Bishop

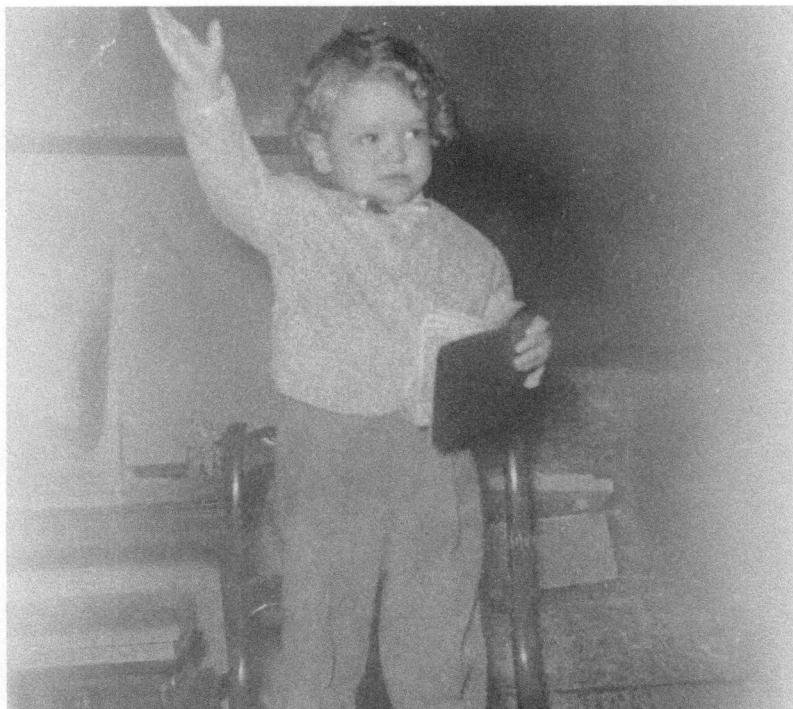

Eldred, the young preacher

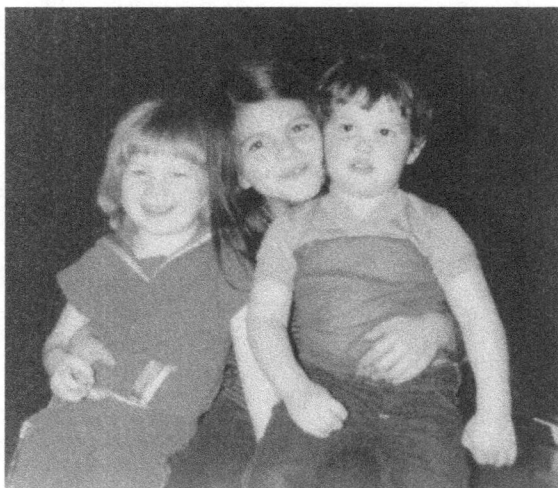

The three children we lose in addiction

Second best day of my life!

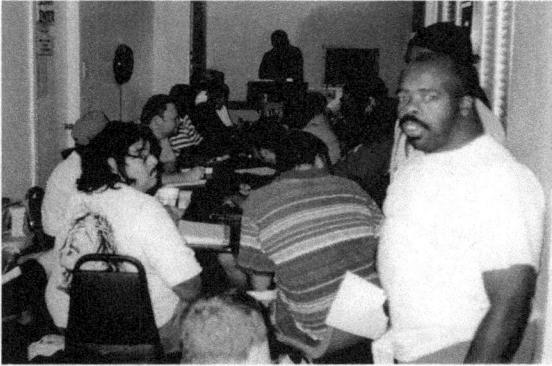

Men's Home using the space we had

CareCenter Thrift Store

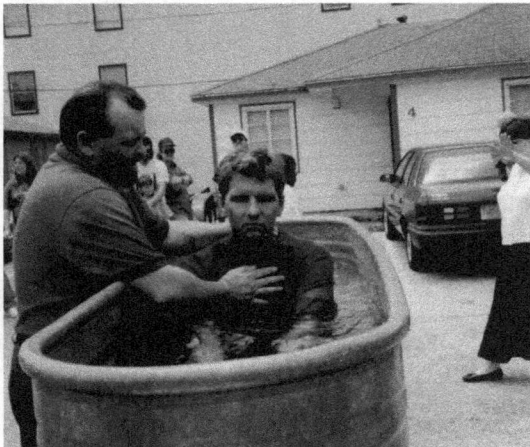

Horse trough baptisms at Eastside

Projects Outreach–The Lord's Angels

Nancy & Joe Martin

Me teaching at the men's home

Robert & Joann Summers

1989: Thursday night outreach where the church began.

Found this man stripping wire in a vacant building and ministered to him

Sweat equity: restoring what the Lord had given us

Restored building

Landon Spradlin & Jimmy Wallace—back bones of our early outreach music

Jimmy Wallace: Dallas guitar legend & regularly played our outreaches

Early women's home & some of their children

First Thanksgiving Outreach

Pastors Terry & Susan Moore ministering in our first home, 1998

Women's home first fruit, Pam Gipson

In New York

Eastside property outreach.

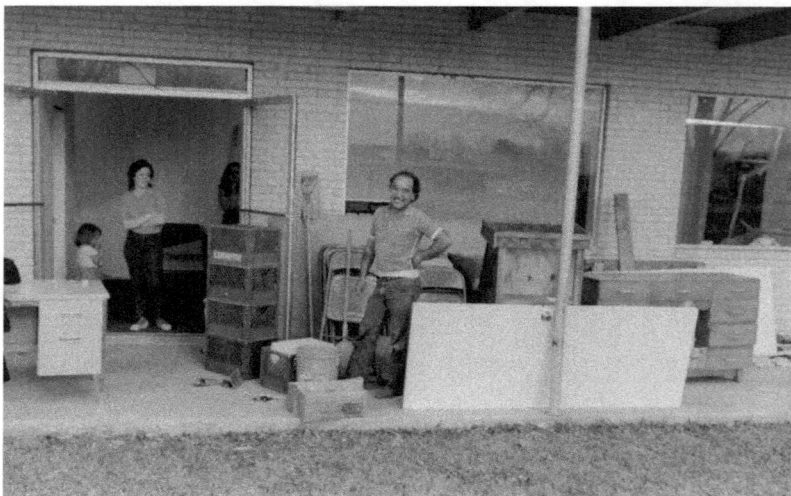

First CareCenter storefront & food pantry

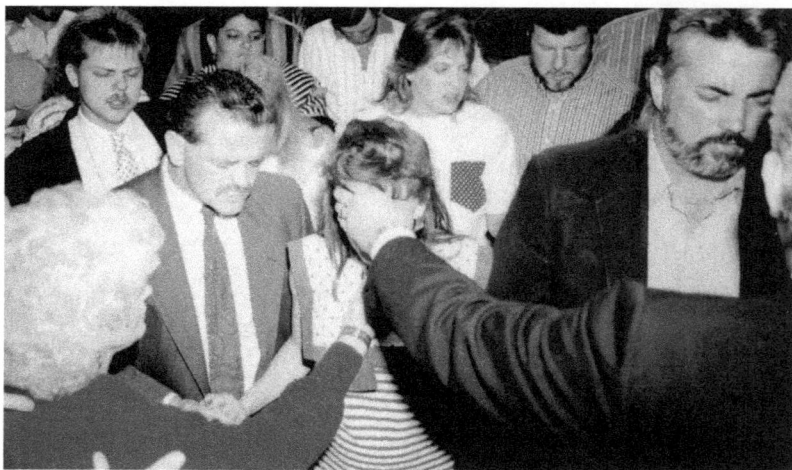

Church on the Rock "send out" to the inner city

Send out for church plant

First "friend-raiser" hosted by our men & women homes

Me & Pastor David Wilkerson in New York, 1988

Ordaining my son Lonnie

First Aim Academy Graduation. Don Hoyt, Frank Robards, Ron White

Men's home, 1988

Firehouse: Leonard and I leading worship

Me and my baby

Early preaching

ELDRED SAWYER grew up in Pleasant Grove and knows first-hand the hardships of poverty, addiction and fatherlessness. His testimony grew into a passion for bringing others to complete restoration through Jesus Christ. As Co-Founder of CareCenter Ministries, Eldred has more than thirty five years of hands-on experience in discipleship, mentoring and missionary work. He has spent more than a quarter-century leading a dedicated group of missionaries to serve the inner-city of Dallas.

Subsequently, he has planted, developed, and oversees CareCenter branches in multiple locations, and is expanding nationwide. Eldred serves on the Board of Directors for four separate non-profit organizations. Additionally, he was selected to serve on the City of Dallas Planning and Urban Development Advisory Committee for the Pemberton Hill Strategic Action Plan. Eldred, affectionately known as "Pops" and his loving wife, Jeanmarie, are proud parents and grandparents to their beautiful family.

www.ingramcontent.com/pod-product-compliance
Lightning Source LLC
Chambersburg PA
CBHW032225080426
42735CB00008B/715